The Harley in the Barn

The Harley in the Barn

More Great Tales of
Motorcycle Archaeology

TOM COTTER

FOREWORD BY PAT SIMMONS

Guitarist for the Doobie Brothers

First published in 2012 by Motorbooks, an imprint of MBI Publishing Company, LLC, 400 First Avenue North, Suite 300, Minneapolis, MN 55401 USA

Motorbooks titles are also available at discounts in bulk quantity for industrial or sales-promotional use. For details write to Special Sales Manager at MBI Publishing Company, 400 First Avenue North, Suite 300, Minneapolis, MN 55401 USA.

To find out more about our books, visit us online at www.motorbooks.com.

ISBN-13: 978-0-7603-4234-3

                        The Library of Congress has cataloged this book as follows:
Library of Congress Cataloging-in-Publication Data

Cotter, Tom.
The Harley in the barn : more great tales of motorcycles archaeology.
    p. cm.
 Summary: ""Harley in the Barn is a narrative and photo-driven book detailing over 35 incredible "barn-finds" of rare and vintage motorcycles from around the world"—Provided by publisher"—Provided by publisher.
 ISBN 978-0-7603-4234-3 (hardback)
 1. Motorcycles—Collectors and collecting. 2. Motorcycles—Conservation and restoration. I. Title.
TL444.2.C677 2012
629.227'5--dc23
                        2012013090

Publisher: Zack Miller
Editor: Jordan Wiklund
Design Manager: James Kegley
Layout: Brenda C. Canales

Printed in China
10 9 8 7 6 5 4 3 2

DEDICATION

This book is dedicated to all the men and women of our armed forces, who fight overseas for our freedom, then often face huge obstacles and challenges when they come home.
Thank you.

Contents

FOREWORD

By Pat Simmons

All of us have heard stories about some obscure vehicle, motorcycle, or car that was squirreled away in the distant past by some eccentric farmer, driver, or collector, and left nearly forgotten for decades. Underneath a dusty canvas tarp, back in the corner of some darkened garage or barn, there it sits, waiting for someone to rediscover it. It's the dream all collectors live for. We always have our ear to the ground, following up on stories, rumors, clues, for-sale ads in magazines, newspaper want-ads, Internet chat, stories from other collectors, or even strangers who knew someone who owned something that they remembered seeing years before.

For those of us who have been hopeless collectors for most of our lives, we have our own stories to tell about how we followed up on a tip or an ad, and ended up lifting the corner of a cover to find a treasure beyond our wildest reckoning. The tales we tell are varied; sometimes mad, occasionally dripping with suspense, melancholy, humor, and even mystery. Often we have found ourselves traveling long distances, searching through crowded suburban neighborhoods or country lanes where you can see only an occasional rooftop through the dense forest. Foraging deep into the inner city, winding within the industrial maze of warehouses in the rustbelt, the ever present image of the Holy Grail etched into our psyche, egging us on, afraid we will miss out on the big find, or that what we find might actually be beyond our means. What about the old car or motorcycle that has been sitting right down the street in the old dilapidated garage we passed every day for the last 20 years, right under our noses! And how many dozens of wild goose chases have we experienced? Still the search goes on.

Our tales are colorful, filled with interesting anecdotes about the most astonishing discoveries. But along with the narrative we have to tell of our own exploits is the unique story behind every amazing vehicle that has made its way into our lives. We celebrate the miraculous technology, inventiveness of individuals, and engineering of an earlier time that allowed these marvels to be produced in the first place. We yearn to know more of the original owners, who, we imagine, were drawn, like us, to the object of our search, and ask as many questions as we can to find out their history and how they came to be the caretakers of these sacred treasures. Their histories become part of ours, and we are forever linked with them and these wonderful machines that have stirred our passions in such delirious ways. For us, spirits dwell within these castings, sheet metal, rubber, glass, wiring, cloth, leather, spokes, and wheels. They speak to us with a voice we can hear across the years.

Many years ago, while on a musical tour traveling through Michigan, I chanced to pick up a local newspaper in a small town. At the time I had a small motorcycle shop in Santa Cruz, California, and I was constantly on the hunt for old bike parts. I went straight to the classifieds and noticed an ad for an "Indian Motorcycle for sale." I called, and the lady who answered the phone said I could come on over and have a look if I would like to. I asked the driver of our equipment truck if he could give me a ride over, and off we went. I was just hoping there would be enough of a basket case there to be able to harvest some parts for a friend who was trying to complete his '46 Indian Chief.

When we reached the residence in an older suburban neighborhood and knocked on the door, we were greeted by an old lady and her daughter. They were nice and invited us in, and took us out to the garage. "This here motorcycle is the last thing my husband was working on before he died," she said. "He just finished it and passed on a few days later." I was not going to find the parts for my buddy's '46 Chief, but there in the corner was the proverbial blanket covering the shape of a motorcycle. When I lifted it, I saw the most beautiful 1941 Indian Four I had ever seen! In fact, it was the first fully restored one I'd ever chanced on. Gulp . . . could I buy it? "If you promise to keep it, ride it, and respect it, the way my husband did, and you have the money to pay for it, it's yours." My heart leapt to my throat. We made the deal, began to roll the bike out, and were about to push it up the ramp into the truck. "Mama, maybe he'd like to look at Billy's old bike?" Huh? "My husband built another bike for my son who was in a wheelchair," she said. "It has a sidecar, but he built it so it could be driven using all hand controls. My husband wanted to be able to go on rides together with my son who was a paraplegic."

Another blanket was swept away revealing a fully restored 1947 Indian Chief and sidecar, with an amazing construction of sprockets and bicycle chains that operated all the foot controls on the motorcycle in an eccentric, but otherwise very efficient, way. What were they going to do with this bike? "Well, it's for sale too, but with all that stuff on it, it may not be for everybody. If you buy both motorbikes, I'll knock the price down some." Was I dreaming?

Three weeks later I was back in California unloading the two bikes into the back of my shop, telling the story of their discovery to my partner, Bill. Thirty-five years later I'm telling this story to you, my friend, and just the telling makes my heart beat faster. Unfortunately, I no longer have the Chief and sidecar, but "The Four" is still in my stable. I smile to myself, thinking how much I have come to love this old bike. It's now an old friend that I visit as often as possible. The fat purr of the engine is forever etched into my memory, and no matter where I am or what I'm doing, I can hear that sound in my head, and feel the gentle bounce from the big leaf spring suspension in front. God! What a bike! What a blessing!

You want to know something? I'm not the only one. I'm probably up there on the motorcycle mania scale, but I have come to know so many wonderfully crazy motorcycle collectors throughout my life. And guess what—they're just as obsessive, some even more so, as I am.

So, get ready to read about some amazing adventures that will make you want to stop and inspect every tin building you see in all the backyards of America. You'll never pass an old barn without wanting to stop and peek in a darkened window. You'll be checking the classifieds in Podunk, Louisiana. And let's not even talk about the internet. That's the barn that has no walls, and no end. It's truly a sickness, and thank God there's no cure. I gotta go now—I need to call a guy, about another guy, who knows a guy whose grandfather used to ride an old Harley Knucklehead that he had stored out in the barn. The hunt continues...

Pat Simmons
Founder, Singer, Guitarist for the Doobie Brothers

INTRODUCTION

The only thing I love more than writing these books is meeting the folks I write about, those who share the same passion of unearthing old machines as I do.

As a fluke back in the mid-1990s, I wrote my first barn-find book, *The Cobra in the Barn*, never expecting it to become a series. Now, five books later, I've met the coolest folks.

Gearheads share a common bond. Within minutes of meeting, gearheads enthusiastically begin exchanging information like they've been friends for a lifetime. It's as if we all belong to a fraternity or private club and the password can be transmitted in just a sentence or two.

So it's been with *The Harley in the Barn*. This motorcycle theme, which began with *The Vincent in the Barn*, has been one of the best-selling series I've written. It seems I'd tapped into a new audience of riders. And it's been great meeting this audience in person.

I think the diversity of interests is intriguing. Like the Indian collector who is also passionate about BMWs, or the vintage Harley collector who collects tiny Yamahas as well. In some ways, finding a barn-find bike entitles you to keep and cherish your discovery whether that was your interest beforehand or not.

Bikes have diverse ownership as well. Social and economic levels don't seem to make a difference in this club. I've met 1-percenters and 99-percenters as pals at motorcycle shows and at flea markets as they both sift through greasy parts in an "Everything $1" box.

One guy I really enjoyed meeting was Pat Simmons. Pat is a founding member, guitarist, and singer for The Doobie Brothers. I got to know him as I was writing another book about rock and roll gearheads, but while sitting in an Orlando bar during the interview, Pat revealed that for decades he had loved searching for undiscovered bikes!

Here was a guy who could buy any restored bike he ever wanted, yet his greatest pleasure is to find, purchase, and sometimes restore barn-find bikes. The reason I say "sometimes" is that he often leaves cosmetics untouched and only refurbishes the bikes mechanically.

You can read Pat's foreword and a story about his 1915 Harley in this book.

Since starting this book, I've added a few bikes to the bucket list—a post-WWII Indian Chief, a 1960s-era BMW, and a purple Triumph Bonneville. Anyway, fasten your helmet and enjoy the ride as you turn the pages. And never stop searching.

PS—if you have a great barn-find story, please let me know. Email me at tomcotter@csx2490.com. Thanks.

Tom Cotter

13

CHAPTER ONE

The Thrill of the Chase

A MOTORCYCLE GREATER THAN THE SUM OF ITS PARTS

The Chief left the Springfield, Massachusetts, Indian factory sometime during the latter part of 1948, en route to a small dealership in Dover, New Jersey. The serial number identifies it as approximately the 1,000th Chief manufactured that year.

There must have been something special about that particular bike, because upon arrival, it became the dealer's demonstrator.

Indian didn't often change the design of its motorcycles, and the 1948 model remained the dealer's demonstrator until at least 1950, when a design change made the leading-link front suspension obsolete, giving way to the more contemporary telescoping front fork. In 1951, the three-year-old bike was finally sold to its first official owner, Russell Reed, a resident from the nearby Mine Hill community. Not long afterward, in 1952, Indian pulled the plug on its manufacturing operations, and this dealership—along with most others—closed its doors for the final time.

Reed used the bike sparingly until 1962. With just 24,000 miles on the odometer, he stopped renewing the registration and parked it next to the shed in his backyard. It sat, forgotten, for the next 45 years.

After four decades of neglect, the Chief had deteriorated badly. In 2007, Reed (now an old man) sold the bike to a man named Albert for the value of the scrap—about $50. Albert dismantled the bike in anticipation of a full restoration, but as all antique bike enthusiasts know, the easiest part of a restoration is the disassembly process. In about four hours, a bike can be totally disassembled. But reassembly can take years or even decades.

Albert knew he had a bike potentially worth much more than the mere $50 he bought it for. He dropped the sheetmetal bits off at a friend's body shop for prepping and painting. He stored the larger pieces—the frame, front end, engine, and gearbox—in a makeshift storage locker engineered from an old truck bed and a locked pick-up cap. Albert's logic was that if someone tried to break in to steal the bike parts, the size and heft of the locker would make stealing it impossible. The rest of the parts and pieces were spread around the property. Then Albert began a very slow restoration while trying to resell it.

This is where master vintage bike hunter Al Kelly comes into the story. Kelly, along with his brother Ken, call themselves Crapoholics, as documented in the book *The Vincent in the Barn*. "I was the guy who found it at Albert's," Al said. "I don't think he owned it more than a month or two."

Kelly had heard that Albert had a disassembled Indian for sale. He went to look at the bike, but thought Albert's asking price (which Kelly was reluctant to share) was more than the pile of parts was worth, so he didn't pursue the purchase.

Wanting to make a statement with his Chief, Belits had the bike painted in the most rarely seen of the Indian's four standard colors, Prairie Green. The restoration is outstanding. *Jason Belits*

"But just a couple of days later, I was talking to my friend Jason Belits," Kelly said. "He mentioned that he was interested in buying an Indian project bike."

Belits said, "I told him I had always wanted an early model Indian with the front fender skirts. In that case, Al told me, I was looking for a pre-1950 model.

"With a smile, he said he knew where there was a 1948 Indian Chief for sale."

Belits went home that night and pitched the Indian project bike to his lady, Amy. Together they decided that if he wanted the bike, he'd need to sell his other projects: a 1951 Triumph chopper, 1952 Harley-Davidson Servi-Car, and 1970 Sportster café racer.

The next day, he and Kelly jumped in the truck and made tracks over to Albert's house. "On the way to Albert's house, I told Al that I had never even sat on an Indian Chief. I was planning to ride it, and was worried that because I am a tall guy, that the bike would be too small for me," Belits said. "So we took a detour and stopped at a friend of Al's who also had an Indian. When I sat on it, it was perfect.

"When we got to Albert's, he showed us the 'security system' and the parts strewn all over his property. Thankfully all the hard-to-find parts—such as the headlight, speedometer, and Indian-face front fender light—were there. He had begun restoring it but had only the valves redone in the motor.

"I told Albert I wanted the bike, and he made it clear that there would be no discussion," Belits said. "The price was firm." Belits was strapped—he didn't have enough cash for the bike until he sold off his other projects. "He said I could take it or leave it, but he would work with me on the timing of the sale. He wanted to go on vacation and he needed some money. So I purchased the sheet metal and made arrangements to square up with him on the balance when he returned."

Belits put his other bikes on the market, but the sales still took longer than he had hoped. He borrowed the balance of the money and completed the purchase. Once he owned the Indian, it sat untouched in his garage for nearly a year until he got his finances together.

In early 2009, the Servi-Car and Sportster finally sold. Belits dropped the Indian off with restorer Dennis Craig, who specializes in Indians. The engine and gearbox were completed immediately, and work progressed as money became available.

"We discussed color," said Belits. "Dennis told me only four colors were available in 1948: Indian Red, black, blue, and Prairie Green. Most folks have their bikes painted either red or black, but he told me that he had never painted one Prairie Green in all the years he had worked on Indians." He decided to paint it Prairie Green.

About a year later, Belits was home when he heard a motorcycle pull up outside. He looked out the window and saw that it was Craig, sitting on the restored green Indian Chief.

"I ran outside, but Dennis took off," Belits said. "So I jumped on another bike and took off after him. When I got to his house, a couple of miles away, I saw my bike, finished at last. And I took my first ride on *my* 1948 Indian Chief."

PATIENCE AND PERSEVERANCE ARE HIS SECRET WEAPONS
1939 Indian Four

One vintage bike enthusiast has the patience of a saint and the tenacity of a bloodhound—two traits that helped him chase a 1939 Indian Four for 23 years before adding it to his vintage motorcycle collection.

His name is Dave Minerva. Like other collectors, Minerva has bought a lot of bikes through classified ads, online forums, eBay, and recommendations of friends, but his discovery and pursuit of the Indian is a barn find on an epic timescale.

A retired electrician, Minerva joined the Seaboard Chapter of the Antique Motorcycle Club of America (AMCA) in 1984 and began networking to find old bikes. "A longtime member named Bob Royal," he said, "told me he knew of an Indian hidden away in an old gas station on the Black Horse Pike. When I asked him which station, he just smiled, looked at me, and said, 'Go ahead, try to find it.'"

Excited by the challenge of a good hunt, Minerva set out to cover the Pike's 60-mile length from Camden, New Jersey, to Atlantic City with his wife and two daughters in the car. Over the course of a day, the family visited every gas station along the route until he discovered the Indian Four. It was hidden in a junk pile inside a BP station.

It was a numbers-matching 1939 model with the original 1265cc four-cylinder engine, styled in that year's popular New York World's Fair paint scheme. Ray, the bike's owner, told Minerva the Indian was not for sale—a statement he repeated every time Minerva stopped by the station for dozens of follow-up visits.

On a cool day in October 2006, 22 years after he first met Ray, Minerva made his way to the gas station once more. "I was out riding, saw the shop, and decided to give Ray another chance to sell," he said. "When I pulled up, there was a dumpster outside the station, and it looked closed. I didn't have any way to leave a message, so I drove back the next day to see if anyone was around. Ray lived in a house next to the station, but no one was there. I had forgotten to bring a business card or something to write on, so I made the trip again the next day." Minerva left a business card on each door of the station and one on the door of the house. He put a letter in the mailbox explaining that he wanted to buy the Indian.

No reply.

By this point in the campaign, most collectors become discouraged and give up, but Minerva was not to be ignored.

"A couple of weeks later, I went back and left cards and a letter again," he said. "Two weeks went by and I finally received a call from Ray's son, sometime in December. Ray had gone into a nursing home, and his son had the Indian

This decrepit BP station in New Jersey was home to Minerva's '39 Indian Four for decades, where it was protected by the pile of junk that surrounded it. Minerva visited nearly every gas station on the Black Horse Pike to locate it.

It took Minerva 23 years to purchase the '39 Indian Four. Although faded, the bike is colored in the popular '39 Indian color combination, commemorating the 1939 New York World's Fair. Although covered with a light coating of surface rust, the bike is in remarkably good shape. It sat for so long that the front tire disintegrated.

at his house. I rode out that day to look over the Indian and make an offer, but the son wasn't sure what he wanted to do with it."

In August 2007—nine months after Minerva discussed buying the bike with Ray's son—he received the call he had been anticipating for 23 years.

"His son was ready to sell and told me, 'Come out Sunday at four o'clock.'

"I met him at his house and wound up negotiating with his wife on the deal. All the local boys were giving lowball offers, so I made a respectable bid and was finally able to bring it home."

1947 Harley-Davidson FL

While 23 years is an extremely long amount of time to close a deal on a motorcycle, it wasn't Minerva's only experience with long negotiations.

In 1987, he was wiring a giant waterslide pump at the Sesame Place theme park in Langhorne, Pennsylvania, when a plumber at the job site told him about an old Harley-Davidson Knucklehead his grandfather bought new in 1947. It was an FL with the 1200cc V-twin with Flanders handlebars, and Minerva was interested to hear that the plumber's cousin, Harold, had inherited it but was not doing anything with it. It sounded like an easy target.

With the cousin's name and city to go on, Minerva looked him up through directory assistance and contacted him about buying the Harley. Harold told him the bike was at his son's house but that he would gladly get it running and discuss a sale.

"I practically had that one in the bag," Minerva said, "until Harold's son had a fit about the bike leaving the family; he wanted it. We had agreed on a $7,000 price, but the son put the kibosh on our deal."

About 10 years later, Minerva was at a swap meet when he saw a red '47 FL with Flanders handlebars—the exact bike he had tried to buy from Harold. Even though the son wasn't there, bumping into Harold and his wife at that event did not go well. "She turned to her husband," he said, "and told him, 'This is the guy who was trying to steal our motorcycle.'

"I took some offense to that because the bike had been worth about $7,000 10 years earlier, but some 'expert' told them it should bring more like $20,000. On that day I met them at the swap meet, it probably *was* worth that much, but not at the time of the first offer."

But Minerva was patient and tenacious. To keep alive the possibility of a deal, he called the couple a few months later and explained the misunderstanding

This is the 1947 Harley-Davidson FL that Minerva was once accused of trying to "steal," although not literally. After 22 years of careful pursuit, it is now in his collection.

of the bike's value. Harold's wife seemed to accept his explanation, and Joe contacted them off and on for several years, just to keep track of the '47.

Around 2009, he phoned and asked if he could visit Harold and the Harley. "I jumped on my '41 Harley with the sidecar and drove out to see them," Minerva said. "Harold was thrilled to death to see that rig. He asked what I thought the '47 was worth, and I told him my honest opinion. I could tell he was starting to soften about selling, but the problem was he had two sons and also felt it should stay in the family for them."

Minerva did not push the matter but visited Harold a few months later, this time on his '68 Harley. He invited the couple to see his collection, which gave them a new appreciation for his enthusiasm of all things two-wheeled.

After touring his bikes, Harold and his wife drove away but returned in five minutes, knocked on Minerva's door, and asked, "How much did you say the '47 is worth?" They discussed the sale more, and before they left, he made sure they both thought the dollar figure was appropriate, just so there could be no misunderstanding.

"A week later," he said, "she called and told me it was my lucky day. I bought the FL on May 12, 2009, or about 25 years after I first heard about it."

1904 Minerva

Another chase that took 20-plus years to conclude involves an unusual foreign make—the kind that Minerva usually avoids. The Belgian company Minerva (no relation) earned a good reputation in the first decade of the 20th century, first as a producer of bicycles, then as a maker of clip-on engines for bicycles, and finally as a motorcycle and luxury automobile manufacturer. The reliability and performance of Minerva engines were such that Triumph imported and used them on its first motorcycles.

"There was a 1904 Minerva in Columbus, Ohio, in the mid-1980s that I tried to buy," he said. "The guy who got it owned an antique furniture store, and he displayed it there for many years."

As always, Minerva's patience for a deal paid off. Twelve years later, the bike was up for sale and he got into a bidding war with Al Doerman, a motorcycle collector of some fame in the Ohio area. He stopped at $7,000 and lost the sale to Doerman at $7,500.

His luck changed, though, when the identities of the bidders were revealed. They were friends. "Al did not know he had been bidding against me," he said, "so he immediately offered it to me after the auction. A lot of rare foreign makes—especially the really early ones—do not have much value in the U.S., so I was afraid to pay more than seven. I offered him a bike of similar value as a trade, but Doerman did not take the deal."

In 2008, Doerman's friend Jim "Scooter" Fronz approached Minerva at the annual Davenport, Iowa, AMCA show and told him Doerman was in a nursing home and selling the Minerva. He was offering it to Minerva for what Doerman had paid for it: $7,500. By now Minerva was confident the bike was worth the price and decided he'd waited long enough.

"I stopped in Columbus on my way home from the show and picked it up," he said, closing another decades-long pursuit.

ROCK AND ROLL BARN-FINDER

Like so many teenagers, two passions consumed young Pat Simmons' life 40 years ago: rock and roll, and motorcycles.

Both Simmons' parents were teachers, so as a youngster he was often cared for by a babysitter. That babysitter was also a piano teacher, which brought music into Simmons' life at an early age. At 6 years old, he picked up the guitar and began singing and strumming. Simmons was playing in coffee shops in the San Jose, California, area by 1963. He was 15.

To support his music habit, he worked in a local gas station, "back when gas stations actually worked on cars," he said. He had always been fascinated by cars and bikes, so when his father's 1953 Chevy needed an engine rebuild, Simmons volunteered.

"The mechanic at the gas station said he would help me rebuild the engine, and teach me at the same time," said Simmons, now 64. "I broke the engine down, reground the valves, honed the cylinders, installed new piston rings and new gaskets. It allowed me to cut my teeth and see what the inside of an engine looked like."

Soon after, Simmons was attending San Jose State University, studying psychology, and playing gigs on weekends with a group called Scratch.

At one of those gigs, Simmons was introduced to fellow musicians: singer and guitarist Tom Johnston, bassist Dave Shogren, and drummer John Hartman. The four decided to form a band, and the Doobie Brothers were born.

The Doobie Brothers played gigs in and around the San Francisco Bay area. They began to pick up a following of motorcycle clubs—and gangs—who enjoyed their music. They often played at a bar in the Santa Cruz Mountains called Chateau Liberté, a favorite hangout of the Hell's Angels.

Compelled by the bike scene, Simmons began looking for his own motorcycle. A friend let him borrow a Honda 305 Dream, and later a 350 Scrambler. Simmons liked riding, but had no money to buy a bike.

Simmons' friend knew of a bike that was being given away. "If you go up to northern California, I know where you can pick up a BSA 441 Victor up in Crescent City. You can have it."

Dazed by his incredible luck and a newcomer to the reality of "free" motorcycles, Simmons and his friend headed north. "I drove my MGB-GT to Crescent City, thinking I could just kick start the bike and ride it home while my friend drove the MG." When they got there, they discovered the bike had been completely disassembled. Why? "Because," the owner said, "it wouldn't start."

So Simmons and his friend loaded the frame, engine, and boxes of parts into his MG hatchback and drove it home. "We had to tie down the hatchback's door with rope because the frame was hanging out of the rear end," Simmons added.

Along the way, he stopped at a BSA dealer and purchased a shop manual for the bike. Within three weeks, the bike was running, which was a challenge because the only tools Simmons owned were a crescent wrench, a pair of pliers, a pair of locking pliers, and a couple of screwdrivers.

It was 1969.

"We played at the Chateau," he said. "We all wore leather jackets, I rode my BSA, Tommy [Johnston] rode a Norton, and soon we got the reputation of being a biker band. We lived that image for a while."

Simmons became infatuated with vintage American motorcycles: Harley-Davidsons and Indians. In 1976 he and a friend opened a shop called Classic Motorcycles of Santa Cruz. They specialized in stockpiling and selling bolt-on pieces for Harley Flatheads, Knuckleheads, Panheads, and Shovelheads. He was clearly way ahead of the curve in the vintage motorcycle hobby.

Like his music career, Simmons was passionate about trends before most others. While many saw old motorcycles as almost worthless, Simmons saw them as history worth preserving. Today, recovering old bikes has become an industry, as they demand high prices in the collector hobby.

To decorate his storefront, Simmons decided he needed a few old bikes. "I heard about a guy who was selling four old Harleys—a 1917, 1922, 1925, and a 1929—and I paid $2,000 for the lot," Simmons said. He was mesmerized by the old American iron. Today, the price of those vehicles is much, much higher.

He began reading and studying motorcycle history. He chased barn-find bikes around the country, mainly using *Hemming's Motor News* as a source. Mostly he enjoyed sniffing out and buying old bikes. He wasn't trying to make a ton of money. "I'd buy a bike for $5,000 and sell it for $5,200 and feel good about it," he said. "It would pay our light bill."

"We'd go to a town for a gig and sit around a hotel and be bored. So I'd open up the local newspaper or *Hemming's* and look for old bikes in the area. If I bought something, I'd put it on the tour truck and bring it home when the tour was over."

Double Indian Deal

As the Doobie Brothers became more popular, Simmons had more disposable income to buy interesting vintage bikes. Once, around the beginning of the Reagan area in 1980, he saw a classified ad in the paper for a 1941 Indian Four. He called the woman who owned it and made an appointment to see it.

"I went over there and she said she was trying to sell her late husband's motorcycle," Simmons said. "She said, 'This is the last motorcycle he ever worked on before he died. This was his project and he was in the process of restoring it when he passed away.' She gave me a price and I said that sounded great."

As he was leaving with his new discovery, the woman's daughter asked if he was interested in another old bike they had. "We have this motorcycle over there," she said. "We are not advertising it. It's a little bit funny and weird."

Simmons' ears perked up. He went over and lifted up the tarp. It was another Indian, a 1947 Chief with a sidecar attached. "It had all these sprockets and chains attached to the handlebars," he said. "It turns out their son was a paraplegic and he couldn't walk."

"My husband built this for my son so they could ride together," she told him.

Her husband had rigged everything so their son could operate the bike using only his hands. The sidecar made joint trips possible.

Simmons and the woman agreed on a price of $4,000 and he loaded that bike in his tour rig as well.

He sold the Chief, but has kept the Indian Four in the corner of his garage ever since. "I haven't run it in years," he said. "I took the tanks off because they were getting rusty. But I'm sure it would still start."

Cris Sommer Simmons proudly stands next to the unrestored 1915 Harley-Davidson her husband, Doobie Brothers singer and guitarist Pat Simmons, found in a barn more than 30 years ago. Cris rode the bike in the 2011 cross-country Cannonball Rally. *Pat Simmons*

Cannonball Bike

"My best barn-find story is the 1915 Harley that my wife, Cris, rode on the Cross Country Cannonball Rally in 2011," Simmons said.

It was 1981. Simmons' friend Mark Allen called. "I just got a line on a guy in Michigan who has a bunch of bikes for sale," Allen said. "Interested in flying up there to take a look?"

Simmons thought that sounded like fun. "So in the middle of winter, we flew to Michigan, where it was cold and there was snow on the ground," he said. "We pulled in front of this guy's house and there were all these Sears kit sheds in the front and side yards. We knew we must be in the right place."

The seller opened crammed building after crammed building, but didn't offer up the bikes—nothing was for sale except for a bunch of rusty parts. Disgusted, Simmons walked back to the car, but Allen continued to talk to the man.

"None of the neat stuff was for sale," said Simmons. "The guy was kind of crabby, as a lot of those guys are. But he was a real hoarder." Simmons and Allen flew home.

About a month later, the seller called Allen and offered him a dismantled 1915 Harley. Allen agreed, but only if the seller assembled it first. The seller agreed, and soon the Harley was in Allen's hands. Simmons congratulated his friend on his good fortune.

A few months later, Allen called Simmons one night and asked if he'd be interested in purchasing a 1915 Harley-Davidson.

"What?" Simmons asked.

"I need the money," replied his friend.

So they made a deal. Simmons traded a 1924 Henderson, a rusty 1920s Indian Scout, plus some cash. In return, he got the 1915 Harley.

The bike featured some of its original coat of paint, and was still in sound condition. Simmons fired it up and put it in the garage, "where it sat for 30 years before we woke it up for the Cannonball," he said.

Simmons' wife, noted motorcycle historian and journalist Cris Sommer Simmons, decided to enter the 2011 Cross Country Cannonball Rally. The only requirement was that the bike be manufactured prior to 1916.

The 1915 Harley came out of its long hibernation. The husband-and-wife team tore the bike apart and sent it to famed restorer Steve Huntsinger. He rebuilt the motor and repaired the frame tubes, which were badly corroded.

"We removed the headlight and horn, because they were so valuable, and substituted a modern LED lamp for the front," said Cris. "But I ran with the speedometer that Pat bought for me for my birthday that year." It was May 2011.

Pat and Cris assembled the bike and took it for a 10-minute test drive. Satisfied, Simmons loaded the bike in a van and kissed his wife good-bye and good luck. She hit the road, heading east toward Kitty Hawk, North Carolina, only to turn around and ride back again, but this time on the Harley. Simmons couldn't join her because he was on tour with his band

Forty-five Cannonball bikes left Kitty Hawk that bright May morning, bound for the west coast 3,000 miles away.

A few days into the Rally, Simmons' concert tour ended and he was able to join his wife's support team on the road.

The group of historic motorcycles averaged 43 miles per hour and completed the ride to California in 16 days. Cris had a hard time keeping up, and couldn't figure out why until she discovered a few of the faster bikes had stroked engines. Hers was stock. "It was the ride of my life, though" Cris said. "And I came in 20th. All I wanted was to finish."

Not too bad for an old Harley.

BORN A RAMBLING MAN

What job provides the best opportunity to seek out old motorcycles during work hours?

Retirement may provide the most free time, but when it comes to legal access to hidden or private property, being a police officer, delivery man, landscaper, or home-improvement specialist is hard to beat.

Add trucking company salesman to that list.

Dicky Panuski, 56, of Davidson, North Carolina, has been in the trucking industry most of his adult life. Even though he lives on the east coast, he spends much of his time selling trucking services in rural areas in Texas, Oklahoma, Mississippi, and Louisiana, areas he says are ripe with undiscovered bikes and parts stashes.

Panuski's *modus operandi* for finding forgotten bikes is to drive into an old town and search out a long-established motorcycle dealership. Once he finds a shop, he walks into the back and asks the mechanics whether they know of any old bikes in the area. Mechanics, he says, are much more likely to know of retired vintage bikes than the salesmen or dealer management.

If there is no motorcycle dealer in town, he visits old lawn mower repair shops. Again, he said, small engine repair mechanics often work on or know of older bikes.

Panuski spent much of his youth riding various two-wheeled vehicles around his Louisiana hometown. His first bike was a Sears moped, which he owned as a kid in the 1960s. He graduated to a Honda 50, then in his early twenties bought a Honda 450, a Honda 750. He left the world of riding for several years, but when he became a police officer, he got back into it. "I joined the police department in Benton, Louisiana, in 1977," Panuski said. "When they started a traffic division, I thought that would be neat, so I rode a police bike for a few years."

His personal bikes included a series of Harleys, beginning with a brand-new police model Fatboy that he purchased through his department. It was solid white when it was delivered, but almost immediately, he began stripping and customizing it. He loved the bikes, but there was always something more he wanted from them; he just couldn't put his finger on what was missing.

Various Fatboys followed until one day he had the opportunity to ride an older bike. Then everything changed. "Once I sat on and rode a vintage bike, I never owned another late-model bike again," he said. "I haven't had an electric-start bike since the early 1990s."

That first vintage bike was an Indian, and he's been hooked on them ever since.

Picking through these shelves, Panuski found a carburetor, exhaust pipes, and miscellaneous hardware. Before he left with his new project, he had found all the major parts. *Dicky Panuski*

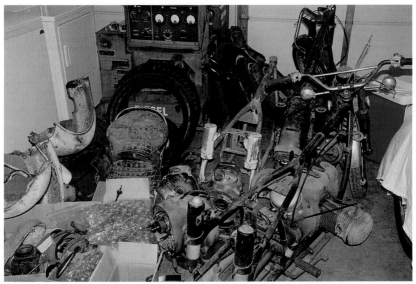

Dicky Panuski knew the man had a barn full of drag racing Harley-Davidsons on the farm near Lufkin, Texas, but when he walked into the "Indian" shed he was treated to this 1947 Chief. The good news was that virtually everything in that particular shed belonged to the Indian. The bad news is that it was pretty sloppy. *Dicky Panuski*

Hey, Honey, Let's Go Camping!

"After I had ridden the Indian, I wanted one real bad," recalled Panuski, leaning on the work bench in his well-equipped garage. "I started to put out feelers for an old bike and had heard about one in Lufkin, Texas. But my wife, Kathy, was getting kind of aggravated because I was spending all my spare time on motorcycles. She said, 'You're not doing anything with motorcycles this weekend!' So I told her 'Let's go camping.'"

The Panuskis got into their motorhome and spent a pleasant weekend in the woods outside Lufkin. Kathy didn't know it then, but her husband's mind was working overtime.

As they pulled up stakes and left the campground on Sunday for the long ride home, he casually mentioned to Kathy, "You know, somebody told me about an old motorcycle, and we're not far from it."

Her eyes rolled. "She told me just not to spend too much time at the guy's house," he said. "She was wise to me."

Panuski pulled in front of the seller's house and was treated to quite a sight. The seller had been a Harley-Davidson drag racer, and had a barn full of Harleys and parts. But when he brought Panuski to a separate barn on the property, Dicky's heartbeat began to rise.

Inside was a 1947 Indian Chief that the man had always promised to restore, but despite 20 years of ownership, never did. "It was all disassembled with the parts all over the shelves," he said. "Engine parts over here, fenders over there."

Within two hours, they struck a deal. Panuski plunked down $5,500 and returned to the motorhome to tell his wife. "'I bought an Indian for $5,500,'" he said. "She asked if she could see it, so I brought her out to the barn."

"Looking at the parts scattered on the shelves, she said, 'You paid $5,500 for that? I sure hope you know what you're doing.'" He loaded everything into the motorhome and brought his new barn-find home.

One of the treasures Panuski found in the piles of rubble was this rare Indian Head front fender light. *Dicky Panuski*

It's hard to believe that only one year earlier, this '47 Indian Chief was a pile of rusty parts in a Texas barn. *Dicky Panuski*

Years earlier, Panuski had owned a couple of prize-winning Cushman and Mustang motor scooters that had been restored by a friend, so he brought the Indian to the same shop. About a year later, his friend called and said the Indian was ready to fire up. "We rolled that bike outside, and it started on the fourth kick," he said. "That was how I got into these Indians. There is something about the vibrations when you ride these bikes."

Like many collectors, as soon as the project was completed, Panuski grew restless. He sold the beautifully restored black Chief and began looking for another project.

"I've owned a dozen, maybe 15 Indians since then, including a four-cylinder," he said. "Unfortunately, I never had the financial wherewithal to go out and buy a bunch of bikes. I always had to sell one to buy the next."

Indian Trader

Panuski moved to Davidson, North Carolina, in 2000 to be near his brother and mother. Soon after relocating, he was riding down a rural road and came upon an old lawn mower repair shop. Panuski stopped and spoke to the elderly man who ran the shop.

In one of old man Moffit's barns, Panuski found these parts for a 1938 Indian; however, other parts were spread around other locations, including a refrigerator and a freezer unit. *Dicky Panuski*

"Do you know anyone around here who is into old motorcycles, particularly Indians?" he asked. The man told him about a fellow named Moffit who built steel industrial buildings, and owned a bunch of Indians and Harleys stored in sheds around his property.

"When I first called Moffit, he was a bit standoffish because he always felt people were trying to cheat him out of his bikes," said Panuski. "So I invited him to come to my house first—so he could see that I was a serious motorcycle restorer and collector."

Lucky he did—"He fell in love with the restored black Indian Chief I owned at the time."

Eventually, Panuski sold the Chief for $25,000 to Moffit. Even though initially there was some suspicion, the two became friends. Moffit finally invited Panuski to come over to his house to see his bikes. "He had shelves and shelves of Indian parts," Panuski said, "and lots of basket case motorcycles. I saw this old, rigid Indian frame and some fenders in the corner. I asked if he had an engine for it, and he said, 'Yeah, it's over there in the refrigerator.' It was a 1938 Indian, and when I found the motor, I asked him if he wanted to

What had once been stored in a chicken coop in the North Carolina mountains had become a show bike. Except for paint, Panuski restored the former Moffit Indian by himself. *Dicky Panuski*

sell it. He said no, that he had found it in a chicken coop in the mountains years earlier and hoped to restore it."

Time went by, and Panuski forgot about Moffit's Indian. Then one day, Moffit gave him a call. "He said, 'I'm over here at the motorcycle swap meet and there is a 1932 Harley-Davidson VL in olive green I'm in love with,'" Panuski said. "He said it was all original but didn't run.

"Then he asked if I was still interested in his Indian. I said yes. So he said that if I brought $6,000 right away to the swap meet, he would use it to buy the Harley, and I could have the Indian."

Panuski said he would be right there. "I keep cash around for just this kind of emergency," he said.

Moffit bought the bike, and about a week later, Panuski went to Moffit's house to collect his new prize. He knew where the frame, fenders, and engine were, but nothing else.

Panuski asked, "Where are the wheels and the brakes?" Moffit told him they were in another building. No surprise, Panuski found the brakes in the freezer unit of another old refrigerator. "It took me six or seven trips to gather up everything for that bike," he said. "But I eventually found everything."

He bought the Indian and restored it within a year.

The Case of the Rare Beamer

Panuski is not exclusively an Indian guy; he's into BMW motorcycles as well.

"I got into BMWs because I really like the German engineering," he said.

A friend had once told Panuski that one of the most desirable BMW motorcycles is an early 1950s R-68 model. "They only made 1,471 between 1952 and 1954," he said. "It was BMW's first sport bike and their first post-war bike that could break 100 miles per hour."

Panuski researched the prefix for the model R-68 serial number—either 650 or 651—and stored it in his brain's hard drive.

Sometime after that, during a particularly heavy North Carolina-to-Texas travel schedule, he stopped into a former BMW motorcycle dealership in Fort Worth. The dealership had closed many years earlier, but the owner was still using the building. He had a bunch of old BMW parts he wanted to sell.

"I was digging through his stuff in the back room and pulled out a bunch of engine pieces," he said. "I started to load the motors into my van when I noticed one case, which was cracked, had the serial number 651103.

It was just one of many BMW engine blocks that were littered across the floor of the old Texas dealership. As Panuski loaded the blocks into his van, there were two things that caught his attention about this block... *Dicky Panuski*

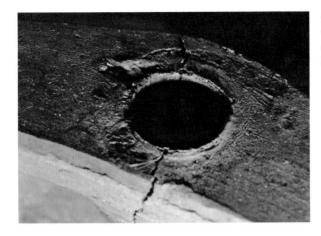

One thing he noticed was that there was a crack in the aluminum block. *Dicky Panuski*

It was a partial motor for an R-68, which I thought was pretty cool." He searched through the rest of the parts but couldn't find anything else related to an R-68.

"I kept that block and brought it to a friend to fix the crack and restore into a complete motor," he said. "I figured if nothing else, I could put it on display. Pretty neat, one of only 1,471."

About a year later, he was scanning the BMW owner's club newsletter when an advertisement jumped out at him. It was an ad for a 1953 BMW R-68 non-matching-numbers motorcycle, with a title, for sale in Butler, Pennsylvania, about 500 miles away.

Panuski called the owner, who informed him that the frame was original but had a later-model BMW engine mounted on it. Again, Dicky's spidey-

But what really jumped out was the serial number— 651103—identifying it as an original engine for one of only 1,471 R-68 BMWs manufactured in the early 1950s. Later, he located an engineless R-68 in Butler, Pennsylvania, with the serial number 651103. He had found the needle in the haystack. *Dicky Panuski*

Admitting that he enjoys the "hunt" more than the restoration process of old bikes, Panuski sent the rare R-68 engine and frame (pictured) to friend Todd Rasmussen in Oklahoma to complete the restoration. *Dicky Panuski*

sense was tingling. "I asked him to read me the serial number on the frame, and he said 651103," Panuski said. "I took the next day off from work and drove right to Butler. It took 10 hours, but I needed that frame. I told him to keep the incorrect engine." The original engine for the bike had cracked many years earlier, so a substitute was installed to get it back on the road.

Once home, Panuski sent detailed photos of the engine and frame to BMW's archives office in Germany. "I sent photos to the factory, and they sent me a certificate verifying that it was built in June 1953 and delivered to a dealership in Germany."

He immediately began restoring his rare find—sending the frame and fenders to a painter—but then the project stalled. "My travel schedule for work just wouldn't allow me the time to work on the bike," Panuski said. "So after about a year of the project just sitting on the shelves in my garage, I called a friend in Oklahoma to finish my project." Shortly thereafter, Dicky owned one of the rarest bikes in the world. The old BMW was restored.

KNUCKLEHEAD DAY

If a rare 1936 Harley-Davidson E model sees its shadow after two decades of hibernation, does it mean another six weeks of storage? It might if the bike is in the neighborhood of Punxsutawney, Pennsylvania.

In 1983, Steve Geiger was a collector on a quest for old motorcycles whose owners did not want them anymore. He had discovered a 1918 Harley-Davidson basket case a few years earlier and developed a knack for locating two-wheeled treasures.

Geiger was in Philipsburg, Pennsylvania, about an hour east of Punxsutawney—home of Phil, the legendary groundhog who has attempted to predict weather patterns each February since 1887. Geiger was in the area not for its proximity to Gobbler's Knob (Phil's home) but to buy a 1936 Indian Chief police bike with original blue paint. He felt it wasn't quite worth the $7,000 the owner was asking.

"I had seen it some years before," Geiger said, "and it looked like a $7,000 bike at the time, but when I saw it in 1983, it wasn't quite there, in my opinion. The owner and I could not come to an agreement, although today I would love to have that bike at twice the price. Probably should have bought it then."

It took sleeping in a freezing cold shed with a pistol, dreaming of groundhogs and surrounded by bears, but Steve Geiger managed to find and buy this 1936 Harley-Davidson. He knew it was a desirable first-year Knucklehead model, but had no idea Harley only built 152 with this engine and frame combination that year.

The bike's owner was nice enough to offer Geiger a shed for the night, and he provided a pistol because that part of the country had an active bear population. Even so, he slept well in the frigid cold night.

The next morning, Geiger went to breakfast in town and watched through the diner window as an older gentleman mowed his yard. Geiger was thinking about the police bike owner's claim that he had already found and bought every old motorcycle in the area. Could it really be true that Philipsburg had no more hidden Harleys or invisible Indians?

He doubted it. After breakfast, he approached the man with the mower. "I asked if he knew of any old motorcycles in garages or barns," Geiger said. "I couldn't believe it when he pointed to the house next to his and said he thought the neighbor had an old Indian that hadn't been ridden for years."

Geiger knocked on the door, introduced himself, and asked the neighbor if he had an old bike sitting around, maybe an Indian. The old man said he didn't have an Indian but there was a Harley in his garage from the 1930s. "I told him that I had a sidecar from that era and asked if he would show it to me."

He said he couldn't because the garage door had not been opened in years and would require digging to get the dirt, mud, and debris out of the way. Maybe Geiger could come back another time.

The Philadelphia-based collector explained he was four hours from home and would have to see it that day, if at all. This made sense to the man, who showed Geiger the shovel and said he would have to do the work.

"I dug out the door and scooted it to the side," Geiger said. "I could see this bike, but it was foggy in there from the light hitting dust in the air.

"I hoped from his description that it might be a VL—the 74-inch V-twin Harley introduced in 1930—but I didn't see the ridge fender of the VL. I used a flashlight to read the VIN, which said it was an E model, meaning it had a medium-compression 61-inch Knucklehead V-twin engine. At the time, I knew that 1936 was the first year for the overhead-valve Knucklehead, so I thought the bike was desirable, but I had no idea at the time that Harley only built 152 of the E models in '36."

For $380 in 1936, the Harley E came with a four-speed constant-mesh transmission, a heavy-duty clutch, 18-inch wheels, twin gas tanks in the saddle fashion, white-face Stewart-Warner gauges, rectangular folding floorboards, a lockable toolbox, and aluminum knuckle-shaped rocker bosses on each cylinder head. By 1983, the value of the vehicle would have skyrocketed.

Boxes were piled around the bike and something was draped over the gas tank, but Geiger—an expert—could see the original paint on this garaged beauty was Venetian Blue with Croydon Cream panels and rims. The bike's owner told Geiger it had been ordered with an optional "porcelainized" paint treatment that made it impervious to scratches.

To show Geiger what he meant, the old man pulled out a key and attempted to drag it down the gas tank. Geiger was so close to owning a nearly perfect example of a first-year Knucklehead that he grabbed the man's arm to prevent the demonstration. "I'm not sure if I shared his confidence in the paint," Geiger said, "and I couldn't take any chances. I told him I would take his word for it and asked if he was interested in selling it. He said he might be."

The owner had been keeping it in hopes that his son would take an interest and want to ride it, but the son had dropped it in the front yard the last time he attempted it. Passing the Harley to his son no longer seemed like a good idea.

Geiger made an offer that the owner accepted, but the title for the motorcycle was somewhere on the second floor of the house and the old man said his wife would know better than he where to find it. His wife was currently in the hospital.

"It would have been useless to pay for the bike and leave with it if I didn't have the title," Geiger said. "I asked if he could give a look for it; otherwise, I wouldn't be able to register it back home." The bike's original title was needed to verify its pedigree. Without it, Geiger couldn't prove the lineage of what he was riding.

He agreed to give it a try, but first helped Geiger load the bike on his truck. While the man was upstairs searching for the title, his son pulled up and asked what Geiger was doing. Geiger explained about the bike sale, which didn't seem to bother the son, who had just stopped by to take his father to the hospital.

Geiger passed the time by having lunch while father and son visited their family member in the hospital. As promised, the owner returned and resumed looking for the title, and the son drove off to work.

Geiger was sure things were going smoothly until 20 minutes later.

"His son came back in a big hurry and slammed on the brakes in the driveway," he said. "He got out of the car and told me, 'Get that bike off the truck!'"

"I said, 'What do you mean? I made a deal with your dad.'"

"He said, 'I talked to my boss, and he said we shouldn't sell that motorcycle, that it's worth a lot of money.'"

"I showed him the bill of sale and told him, 'Look, we've already made a deal.'"

The son kept insisting the bike was no longer for sale, even though his father had been paid for it. Geiger asked him to get his father downstairs so they could all talk about it. Geiger ended up offering the old man an extra $1,000 in cash—another grand on top of the earlier deal was the icing on the cake that won them both over. The son even offered to help the old man find the title.

When he got the bike home, Geiger drained the gas tank, cleaned the carburetor, changed the oil, put in a battery, pumped up the tires, and poured in some gas. The 47-year-old Milwaukee machine fired up and idled as smoothly as a Knucklehead can idle.

"I took it down the road," he said. "I was used to Panheads and bigger bikes; I was riding a '65 Harley daily, but that E was the fastest Harley I had ridden in my life. When I had a chance to clean it up and really look at it, I couldn't believe how nice it was, even after sitting in a dirty garage since the 1960s. Even the leather seat and saddlebags were in excellent condition."

Geiger kept his E barn find in pristine condition for 10 years before selling it to finance another purchase. To this day, it has never needed restoration.

"It had 24,000 miles on the odometer, and I think that '36 Knucklehead was in as good a shape as, or better than, the one that Harley-Davidson has in its museum."

BIKE IN THE BARN
By Doug Kaufmann

It was a 1953 Vincent Black Shadow, but I didn't know it then. All I remember was holding on so tightly to that beautiful black motorcycle that my hands felt like vices. If I live to be 100 years old, I will never forget the roar coming out of what I thought were twin engines.

As we leaned into each turn and he shifted through the gears, the only things that became tighter than my hands gripping under that seat were the muscles in my neck! He was a respected motorcycle restorer and I was a friend of his son, George, and I had just happened to come off of a Los Angeles beach that day long enough to become his back-seat weight for the test drive. A few years later, I learned that I took the back seat on a 1953 Vincent Black Shadow. As it turned out, there was only one engine, albeit a "V-Twin" engine.

Along came marriage, a wonderful family, a great job, and a lot of responsibility. Through it all, I never forgot that test ride and the sounds that V-Twin engine made. As insignificant a part as I played in it, that one test ride left me hungry to relive one of the most significant testosterone shots I had ever experienced in my early years; that mysterious black bike beckoned.

The marriage is going strong after 32 years, the kids are grown and successful, and my career is alive and well. Around the same time that I learned my mother was ill, I received a phone call from a friend apprising me that a 1949 Vincent Black Shadow had just been listed on eBay. I recall thinking, "Sure, like that would ever happen." I knew that these motorcycles were coveted by wealthy collectors and often they were priced about the same as three-bedroom homes in many American cities. But eBay? I was running out to the airport for a flight to see Mom when another friend of many years called me and asked, "Did you know that there is a Vincent motorcycle listed on eBay?" My interest was piqued, and after landing and hugging Mom, I asked to use her computer.

Not only was there in fact a beautiful 1949 Vincent Black Shadow listed, but the seller had a zero feedback rating score. He had never listed nor sold anything on eBay. Those who use eBay know that a zero-feedback listing is a red flag to buyers—zero-feedback sellers are generally not up to speed on how to best list their product or how to communicate with potential buyers. I emailed him a letter inquiring about the motorcycle and did not hear back. Several days later, I wrote him a nice email introducing myself and stating that he must be new to eBay and was probably deluged with inquiries. He responded in kind; his name was Morgan Lodge, and he said his eBay

Kaufmann's childhood dream come true; he is now the owner of an unrestored Vincent! The bike has been refurbished mechanically, but its cosmetics remain original. There can't be many like that remaining in the world today. *Doug Kaufmann*

experience had been a bit overwhelming. He was selling a '49 Vincent; I could see why he was overwhelmed.

We sent a few more emails to each other and I knew that he grew uncomfortable with all of his incoming inquiries. Surely these came from people just like me. Beautiful and highly desired '65 Porsches come up daily for sale on eBay, but an original, low mileage, 1949 Vincent Black Shadow Series C motorcycle comes up once in a lifetime. Morgan was tired of trying to respond to so many people. I was in the right place at the right time. The seller was a true gentleman and he and I agreed on a price. Three days later, I became only the third owner of this magnificent machine. But where our deal ended, this story begins.

There was snow on the ground the night Mom died in early 2010. As the sun rose, my wife and I sat with my siblings and their spouses in our mother's living room, reminiscing about her life. She was our mother, but also our best friend. Throughout her illness I communicated with the seller and told him that spending time with my mother set precedence over picking up the motorcycle. He told me that he well understood since his father was also aging and he would have done the same thing, given the circumstances. He said the Vincent had rested at his house for 55 years and a few more weeks seemed inconsequential.

Following Mom's funeral, my wife flew home and gave me her blessings to drive my rented Subaru 4x4 up through the snow-filled Sierra Nevada Mountains and head toward northern California to get my first glimpse of the Vincent in person. I never recommend buying anything sight unseen, but the buyer was such an honest person, and since he had provided me with thorough documentation of the authenticity of the bike, I decided to gamble a bit. Had I balked in the least, I knew that 100 other vintage motorcycle nuts were patiently waiting right behind me. I jumped.

Hours later, after driving through snowdrifts higher than my car, I ended up in a small California community that I had heard of but had never visited. Morgan told me to pull up to the gate and call him. For the next several hours, my life became surreal. A beautiful home in front hid the rest of the property. Behind the home was another one with a garage and workstation under it. A door under the house revealed a steel tie-down cable where the Vincent had been chained since 1953. Most importantly, I got to meet Morgan's father. Having just lost my mom, it was such a pleasure to shake his hand and to meet the man who, like me, had a passion for this legendary motorcycle and who had stored it, perhaps waiting to hear the roar of that engine one more time, as I had some 40 years earlier. I literally could not believe I was standing there with not only the motorcycle, but with its 55-year owner and his son and wife. While I pined to hear that engine and sit on that Vincent seat again, it felt that this one particular motorcycle sat and quietly waited for me, too. Maybe it was my emotions running wild after Mom's death, maybe it was this wonderful family that I stood with, or maybe I was impacted by this incredible relic, but the experience felt religious.

The Vincent was Morgan's father's treasure, not his. His dad acquired it in 1953 for $350, and then rode it from California to Coos Bay, Oregon. It made the round-trip journey without incident, a testimony to its engineering. Soon thereafter, an engine noise prevented him from riding it anymore, and he opted to store it rather than sell it. For security purposes, he chained it to the anchored cable. And there it sat. As he was drafting his estate plans, his son took ownership of the Vincent. A motorcycle rider himself, Morgan had a beautiful, fully dressed Harley sitting in that same wonderful chamber that also housed the Vincent. Morgan pondered riding the Vincent, so he found the best restoration shop and paid them handsomely to restore it mechanically, but he made the brilliant decision to leave the exterior, with all of its wonderful patina, just as it was during his dad's ownership, including the small dent on the gas tank. I sat down, and it started on the first kick. As I grasped under the seat, I had a deja-vu experience. It was 1969 again, and I was just a kid from the Los Angeles beach. Only this time, I was no longer added weight on the rear end. This was real and I was the test pilot! I pinched myself and realized that this time, it was mine.

We hugged, said our goodbyes, and arranged delivery of this mighty beast of a motorcycle. What an incredible day! As the Subaru entered the snow-covered mountains a few hours later, I felt a strange sensation. It felt like Mom was sitting there next to me in the car. I shut off the radio, enjoying the sensation. Mom always told me that she expected only the best from me. Those words rang in my ears. In the silence, I knew that she would have loved to spend this special day with me. Somewhere in the Rocky Mountains, I finally realized that everything in life is relative; as much as I loved that old motorcycle, I'd trade it away tomorrow for one more day with Mom.

THE BEEMER AND THE CHIEF

Lyle Manheimer's spare time is devoted to the pursuit of motorcycles, which explains how he has discovered so many of them in barns, body shops, and all manner of unusual locations.

Manheimer likes every breed of motorcycle, whether foreign or domestic. He got his first contemporary bike in 1970, a '64 Honda 305, and his first vintage machine, a '47 Indian Chief, in 1976. He performed a full restoration on the Chief, which he bought for $1,500 from a friend who needed cash to buy a 4x4 vehicle. After riding it for five years, he parked the bike in his garage, where it still has tremendous eye appeal.

Joining the Antique Motorcycle Club of America (AMCA) accelerated his passion for two-wheelers, as did the discovery and purchase of a basement full of Indian parts not far from his home.

Sometimes his excitement to play with a new toy gets the better of him and he buys a motorcycle when he already has too many projects lined up. Such was the case with a 1970 Norton Commando S basket case he recently found in a storage container and took home for $750. It seemed like a good idea at the time, but when a fellow club member asked about it, Manheimer

After a lifetime of riding motorcycles, Lyle Manheimer bought his first vintage German bike. This 1965 BMW R50/2 had been sitting in a body shop for years when he heard about it through word of mouth.

let the Norton go for $550 to clear a spot in his garage and give somebody else a shot at it. (To Manheimer's satisfaction, the Norton underwent a beautiful restoration and hit the show circuit at a Perkiomen Valley Chapter of the AMCA event in 2010).

His collection usually numbers around 15 bikes of all types. It currently includes Harleys from the Shovelhead and Evolution eras, several Indians, a Benelli, and a '75 Yamaha.

In 2008, he added an example of the most famous, most successful German motorcycle brand to his garage when he heard about an old BMW for sale. "I've retired from my regular job as an electrician at a major utility in New Jersey," Manheimer said, "and I help a friend out with his motorcycle shop. A customer mentioned he knew of a 1965 BMW for sale and gave me the contact information. I must have called the phone number a half-dozen times without a reply. I had given up on the guy when he finally got back with me. It didn't sound like he was in a hurry to sell the bike."

After another week of back-and-forth phone work, Manheimer and the BMW owner agreed to meet at the body shop where the bike had been stored

BMW motorcycles had an Earles leading link front fork that was designed to limit front-end squat while braking.

The R50/2's engine is a 493cc horizontally opposed air-cooled twin that produces 26 horsepower. It is backed up by a four-speed manual transmission and shaft drive. For many years, BMW was one of the few bike builders using horizontally opposed engine layouts.

for four years. The owner told Manheimer the bike had been running when it was first parked but couldn't make any guarantees about its condition now.

Manheimer arrived at the location on time but had to wait another 45 minutes for the seller to arrive. He could see the bike in the back of the shop, covered in years of Bondo dust. "I think the guy was motivated to sell the BMW because the people at the body shop were tired of seeing it in there," Manheimer said. "When he finally arrived, he had a can of gasoline and a six-volt motorcycle battery. The gasoline worked fine, but the battery was dead."

After a few minutes of charging, the owner pushed the BMW out into the daylight where Manheimer got his first good look at it. It was an R50/2, black, with a 493cc horizontally opposed air-cooled twin that produced 26 horsepower. A four-speed transmission sent power to the rear wheel through BMW's enclosed driveshaft, and the front carried an unconventional (for 1960s America) Earles leading link fork design.

The bike was not in pristine condition; it looked like a 43-year-old BMW that had never been restored. The owner possessed the bike for about 10 years and let a friend ride it one day, resulting in a spill on a gravel road that put a few dings and dents on it. The owner looked at the odometer and said he

Lyle Manheimer found a family selling its late father's 1948 Indian Chief after decades of storage in a barn. It was mostly complete and in decent riding condition, although Manheimer says it received an amateurish paint job and a few minor modifications in its lifetime.

thought it only had 6,000 miles on it. Manheimer pointed to the worn foot pegs and hand grips and general condition and said he was certain it was 106,000 miles. "BMWs are known for longevity," Manheimer said. "Being over the 100,000-mile mark did not bother me if the bike had been given good care and maintenance. I wanted to hear it run and ride it before judging whether or not it was in good shape."

With the weak battery, it took half a dozen kicks to start the engine. Unfazed by its years of sitting, the BMW fired and idled with confidence. The owner rode it around the parking lot, then let Manheimer take a spin to check that all four gears engaged and the clutch felt strong.

When it comes to buying old bikes, Manheimer goes with his instinct, and he had a good feeling about the Beamer. He told the seller that he was still interested.

"He told me he wanted $3,500 for it," Manheimer said. "That sounded fair for what I thought was an attractive motorcycle that seemed to be in good condition, so we arranged to finish the sale a week later at the body shop.

"I still see the guy around. He's a big Harley guy. He always asks me how the BMW is doing; I tell him it's found a good caretaker."

This is not a stock 1948 Indian Chief taillight. When Lyle Manheimer found this bike, it had a few "upgrades" that he can't wait to remedy, such as this utility trailer taillight. Other modifications include a light switch from an old car that is held in place by hose clamps.

"I prefer finding bikes that can be made into good riders with very little work. Since I got the BMW, I've changed the oil, rebuilt the carburetors, and rewired the handlebars, headlight, and horn switch."

Manheimer's enjoyment of the little black Beamer has only reinforced his philosophy that an enthusiast should keep his mind open to all varieties of two-wheeled machines.

"I had never had a German bike before, but I had heard enough good things about BMWs to know they were well built and reliable. This one didn't look like much when I first saw it in the body shop, but now when I want to ride an old motorcycle, the R50/2 is the one I get out of the garage. It never lets me down. I would certainly consider buying another one."

In 2010, Manheimer was again at his friend's shop when a customer said he had a line on a 1948 Indian Chief in a barn. He was trying to help the family that had it raise money because the mother had some medical problems and could use the extra income. Manheimer arranged to see the bike.

A true barn find, the Chief was so packed in with a bunch of junk that Manheimer could not get to the left side of the bike to check the numbers of the frame and engine. "The numbers should match on an Indian," Manheimer said. "On that first day, all I could see for identification was a 1948 gauge cluster, and the front wheel speedometer gear setup told me it was a '48, as well."

Manheimer asked if it ran. The seller, a gentleman in his mid-fifties, said that his father had bought it in the 1960s and rode it often. His father parked it in 1968 when he became ill and passed away shortly after that. The bike had not been removed from the building in 42 years, although the seller had made a habit of starting it occasionally. Clearly, that practice had stopped decades earlier.

When it came time to make an offer, Manheimer explained the factors he used to arrive at his proposed dollar figure. He liked the fact that the bike was an Indian, one of the most desirable vintage motorcycle marques in America, and that it had most of its original sheet metal and parts. What bothered him was the fact that it had sat for so long it was effectively a non-runner, and that someone had installed a few incorrect (and unattractive) components, such as a utility trailer taillight and an old car light switch (held in place by hose clamps). "Taking all of that into account," Manheimer said, "I told them I thought $10,000 was a reasonable offer. I stressed they were free to shop it around and see if someone else would give them more money. I also told them my offer was contingent on their being able to provide the bike's title. It is darn near impossible to register a bike in New Jersey without the proper paperwork. Title services don't cut it here. It would kill the deal if the title could not be found. I would use that paper to verify the engine and frame were original. I gave them my phone number, and they asked me to give them a few days to mull it over."

The deal's middleman called Manheimer three days later and wanted to know if he could go higher on the offer. Manheimer told him that was the top of his comfort zone. The family had looked on eBay and gotten the idea that it was worth a lot more.

"I said it was a fair offer," Manheimer said, "but that they should put it on eBay if they wanted to go to the trouble. There is always somebody willing to overpay for something as desirable as an Indian on eBay, so they might get lucky."

Within an hour, Manheimer received a call from the family accepting his offer. One week later, he took the family the $10,000 in cash and backed his truck up to the building. In daylight, the Chief was a sight to behold.

Manheimer thinks it was originally red but had been amateurishly repainted blue. It was covered with dust and had two flat tires.

Manheimer checked the title against the VIN and verified the bike's originality. He inflated the Indian's tires with a portable air tank so it could be rolled into his truck and relocated to his home.

He didn't jump directly into restoration. His new project is neither an American, British, German, Italian, nor Japanese motorcycle. "I'm focused these days on building a new garage," he said, "which will be set up specifically to be a motorcycle workshop." Once the construction is complete, the '48 Chief will get the attention it deserves.

CHAPTER TWO

Strange Places

SHE SELLS SEASHELLS BY THE SEASHORE

Tourists find a lot of neat mementos in gift shops, but it is the rare souvenir hunter who turns up a desirable 80-year-old Indian Scout motorcycle. Carlos Escudero likes to tell the story of how, in 2011, such a machine made its way to his motorcycle repair shop, Solo Moto, in Greenwich, Connecticut.

"Four years ago, my friend Ian MacMillan was in a store in Mystic, Connecticut, called Shells Galore 'N More, when a lady asked him if he might be interested in something that wasn't on display," Escudero said. "Her name was Erica Hall, and she was the owner. Erica said she had an old boat and a motorcycle she needed to sell."

She showed him the nearby boat, a 63-foot World-War-II-era Coast Guard vessel that was serving as her temporary home while she and her husband built their house in Pawcatuck. The boat was only useful for parts, but she showed him photographs of a complete and presentable 1928 Indian Scout 101.

When introduced as a 1920 model, the Scout was a middleweight cycle powered by a reliable and powerful 600cc V-twin. Designed by Indian engineer and racer Charles B. Franklin, the Scout featured a gearbox bolted to its two-cylinder engine, opposed to earlier gearboxes being mounted separately. Franklin was also responsible for the short-frame Scout Model 101, which was introduced in 1928 with a lower seat, more rake in the fork, and a longer wheelbase than its predecessor.

The Scout was fitted with a front brake, a choice of Indian's 600cc or 750cc V-twin powerplants, and a three-speed transmission. Indian produced the strong-handling 101 for three and a half years before the cash-strapped company consolidated its models into a standard, larger frame.

Finding an example today that isn't modified for racing or stunt work is extremely rare.

"Ms. Hall told Ian that her husband rode the Scout regularly when they married in 1949," Escudero said. "The couple graduated to a larger Harley-Davidson and parked the Indian for good in 1959."

But they held on to the bike all those years. Her husband had recently passed away, and she was hoping to find it a good home. Erica promised Carlos that she would move it first from her old home to her new place in Pawcatuck, then give him a call to talk about selling it. She made it clear she would not be rushed and that she intended to determine its value before accepting any offers. "This went on for about three years," Escudero said. "All the while I stayed after my friend to keep in touch with her. I kept telling him, 'Don't lose this lead!'"

Escudero's patience was rewarded during the 2010 holiday season when the owner invited him to her home near the Rhode Island border to see

Even surrounded by expensive European sport bikes, this 1928 Indian Scout Model 101 grabs everyone's attention. The middleweight motorcycle's green coloring might lead one to think it was military issue, but the truth is it was probably painted in the maintenance yard of the Southern New England Telephone Co. sometime in the 1940s or 1950s.

the Scout. He saw an intact Model 101, standing above a puddle of its own fluids, whose 750cc V-twin showed compression when kicked. He took snapshots, but it would be another seven months before Ms. Hall would entertain an offer.

"Finally, in July of 2011," Escudero said, "she called. We agreed on a price, and she told me to come get it. I told her I would be there the next day with cash, which she said was fine. When I tried to pay her, however, she said having all that money around would make her uncomfortable. I had to get a cashier's check to close the deal."

The only modification Escudero could see was the Scout's color. Erica's husband worked for the Southern New England Telephone Co. (SNET) after his service in World War II. Using the company's maintenance yard equipment, he must have painted the Indian the same greenish hue as SNET's service trucks.

The bike arrived at Moto Solo just before July 4, which is probably the worst time of year for a motorcycle shop owner to get a new toy. "We are really busy in the shop in the summer," Escudero said, "so I could not play with the

Indian right away. But the next day, two friends stopped by, and saw the bike. They told me to call home and tell my wife I would be late for dinner—getting the bike running was their top priority."

But they had their work cut out for them. The crew knew the V-twin had compression, so they turned down the shop lights to see if the magneto had any spark to offer the combustion process. When the Scout failed that test, they hooked up a battery and a conventional ignition coil, running the circuit through the points in the magneto.

With the electrical element of the equation sorted out, their attempt to prime the carburetor ended with gasoline leaking everywhere. Close examination affirmed the carb was gummed up with a stuck float—not an unusual condition for an engine that had been sitting unattended for more than a half-century.

As with most motorcycles from that era, the Indian's gas tank is composed of two separate compartments—one for gas, the other for engine oil—and an oil priming plunger. The tank and everything attached to it needed some level of rehabilitation.

"The tanks on these older bikes always need repair," Escudero said. "The Indian showed a couple of temporary repairs. Nobody ever fixed these tanks exactly as they had been manufactured in the factory, due to the many composite pieces that had to be carefully lead-soldered. Liquid oozed out of the bike from everywhere. With some jury-rigging and a lot of determination, we got the engine to fire up, and we videotaped our efforts and posted them on YouTube. One of us is holding the camera; one of us is holding the battery lead; and the other is manipulating the carburetor by hand.

"When it came to life it was a smoke bomb, and the first run shot sunflower seeds out of the tailpipe. The shop had that aroma everybody expects from an old bike that has sat in a barn for most of its life—part oil, part gas, and part rodent."

Escudero and friends were so encouraged by the smell of burning field mouse that they began prepping it for the upcoming Fairfield County (Connecticut) Concours d'Elegance, which offered a barn-find judging class for cars and bikes with interesting discovery stories. Getting the Scout to riding condition took 40 hours of spare shop time during the busiest two months of the season, and a few hundred dollars in spare parts.

The philosophy behind Solo Moto is that old motorcycles should only be "rehabbed and refurbished" to the point that they can be ridden safely. Too much work kills the history and spoils authenticity, according to Escudero. And this bike was special.

"We deal with every conceivable bike ever made," he said. "At any time, we might have Ducati, Bultaco, BMW, Moto Guzzi, Norton, BSA, or even Brough Superior motorcycles in the shop.

Many hours were spent on the Indian's rehabilitation. There was no attempt to restore the bike to museum quality; its owner (like many barn-find collectors) feels it would erase the machine's authenticity and history.

"This Indian, though, has been a real surprise to all of us. We had never dealt with an old Indian, so working on one of the most desirable and historic models has been a mind-blower. How did we score a bike like this and get it going without having to rebuild it? We are in awe of how incredible this motorcycle—built before World War II, even before the Great Depression—holds up to today's V-twins in terms of engineering and feel."

Riding the Scout has provided Escudero and his friends a window into 1920s-era state-of-the-art motorcycle technology. "I have had it on the road three times," he said, "and it really has quite a personality. It easily breaks 60 miles an hour.

"The only negative is that—like all early bikes—the brakes are just not there. Engineers were trying to iron out the handling and get the engine to work without breaking down, so stopping was not as important to them."

Solo Moto recently held an open house, during which the '28 101 Scout was a magnet for attention. It was displayed in all its barn-find glory while the 2005 film *The World's Fastest Indian* played on a large screen nearby.

The movie's promotional poster reads, "Based on one hell of a true story." Escudero can relate. After all, that tagline also applies equally well to a story about a guy who finds an 80-year-old Indian in a seaside gift shop in New England.

HOW MANY BSAs DOES IT TAKE
TO HOLD UP A FENCE?

Lanny Hyde has some cool bikes. His Vincent Rapide, which he found in a southern California shed, was featured in the book *The Vincent in the Barn*. This time Lanny documents another find, one he refers to as a Desert Sled.

These days, Hyde lives in Oak Hills, California, about 150 miles from St. Helena, where he lived when he received a note from his friend Jack Batson.

"When I lived in Napa Valley, Jack sent me some photos of his latest find," said Hyde. "As it turned out, it was a BSA Gold Star that had been used for years as a fencepost, believe it or not."

Hyde's friend Batson mentioned to a mutual friend—Dave Spilka—that Batson needed a brake arm for his BSA. Spilka is a car picker, and while removing an old car from a backyard in Paramont, California, he spotted an old BSA—brake arm and all—that was holding up a fence. When he asked the owner about it, he was told just to take it, so he loaded it onto his truck and brought it home.

"Spilka immediately called Jack and told him the good news," said Hyde. "He told Jack, 'Hey, I found your brake arm, but the only problem is that it is attached to a motorcycle.'

"Jack asked what kind of bike it was attached to. Dave described a BSA with an alloy cylinder head and barrel. When he read the serial numbers to Jack, he realized it was a Gold Star."

The Gold Star appeared to have a desert racing history. In the southwestern United States, "Desert Sleds" were popular in the early 1960s in places like the Mojave Desert. Bikes like BSA, Matchless, and Triumph were stripped and built as racers for flat-out "hound-and-hare" 100-mile races across the desert, usually in two 50-mile loops. Actor Steve McQueen was known to be a Desert Rat, racing various four-stroke machines all over the Southwest. By the late 1960s, two-strokes like Husqvarna, CZ, and Greeves Challengers began to dominate the desert racing scene, and the traditional Desert Sleds were eventually put out to pasture. Or converted to fence posts. The Gold Star had been a Desert Sled, and was in very rough condition.

Batson sent his friend Hyde photos of his fence-post find. Hyde instantly noticed that the BSA had a Honda gas tank, not surprising given the tough desert service the bike had endured. "The original gas tank was probably damaged while racing, so the owner just installed the cheapest tank available to replace it," Hyde said.

After looking carefully and inspecting the photos, Hyde called Batson and asked what he planned to do with the BSA. "Probably just get it running and sell it," he said.

Hyde actually wanted to race it. He asked Batson if he would be willing to let him restore it and use it as a vintage motocrosser. Batson agreed, and gave the bike to Hyde, free of charge. As they began to disassemble the bike, they were surprised that it was not a 500cc, which they had thought, but instead 350cc.

"These were not as popular as the larger 500cc bikes because the bigger bikes were much faster in the desert races," Hyde said.

Batson rebuilt the engine, installing a new sleeve, piston, and rings, and rebuilt the transmission. In the meantime, Hyde located a proper gas tank in England and a seat "that had seen better days" from a dealer in Fresno.

To complete the vintage look, Hyde found a pair of period-specific, shouldered Akront rims. As per the original specs, he had the aluminum rims polished, purchased new stainless steel spokes, and painted the hubs black. He brought them to a wheel builder, had them laced, and had new tires and tubes installed.

Hyde had the frame powdercoated and a set of Beator forks installed. "Jack fabricated a center-mount oil tank and fender braces, installed the wheels and motor, and the bike was coming together nicely.

"It was evident that this was going to be a cool, premier motocross ride."

Hyde entered his BSA in a vintage motocross in Hollister, California, and enjoyed good results. But he was also concerned about a ticking noise coming from the engine. Then the engine locked up.

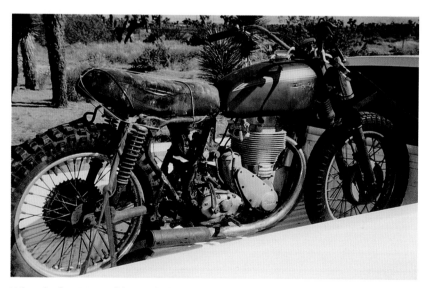

When the free BSA Goldstar, which had been ridden hard in the desert, was taken off fence-duty, this is how it looked. Not pretty, but barn-find pro Lanny Hyde saw a diamond in the rough and decided to give it a full restoration. *Lanny Hyde*

Hard to believe, but this is the same bike. Hyde competes in vintage motocross events with the bike, which he says runs like new. *Lanny Hyde*

"I brought it back to Jack and he removed the head to discover a damaged piston and bent exhaust valve," Hyde said. "Further investigation revealed that the piston had been installed backwards." The exhaust valve was slightly larger than the intake valve and the piston cutouts were slightly different in size.

Jack had done a number of Gold Stars and this had never happened before. He was beside himself.

With a vintage bike race just six days and 1,200 miles away, getting the engine repaired in time didn't seem likely. However, Hyde located a piston and rings in San Jose and had them shipped overnight.

Batson and his machinist Phil Wyatt worked overtime, bored the cylinder, fixed the valve, and reassembled the motor. By the next morning, the Gold Star ran like new, and Hyde departed ASAP for the motocross event in Chehalis.

"It ran great and a good time was had by all," Hyde said. They continued to race the bike in other vintage events.

Not bad for an old fencepost.

JUST GIVE IT A KICK
by Mike Stenhouse

In 1967, I was working as an aerospace engineer at Pratt & Whitney in East Hartford, Connecticut. I lived with several friends in a bachelor house in Manchester. We all had the need for speed. Tom Flaherty, one of the housemates, raced a nice Shelby GT350R. Two of us took up motorcycle racing.

New England was a great place for enduros (cross-country motorcycle speed trials). The countryside is heavily wooded and laced with trails. The New England Trail Riders Association ran enduros on weekends from early spring to late fall. The trails were so challenging that we had to ride wide open in the clearings just to make the 24 mph average trail speed. No wonder that many of America's best International Six Day Trials (ISDT) riders, including some of the guys we rode with, came from New England.

I took a ride up to Willimantic one day to see a gun dealer about a hunting rifle. His shop was at the end of a dead-end dirt road—for good reason, I later found out.

We got to talking and eventually the subject turned to motorcycles. As it turns out he had a motorcycle in the shed behind his store. We went back to look at it. Apparently he had taken it in trade and didn't ride it. Now he just wanted his money out of it.

It had been dropped, the tank was dented, and forks were twisted slightly. It was a Triumph 650—like a Bonneville, but something about it was a bit odd. He wanted $600. I started to offer less, but he quickly interjected, "I sell things on the low end of the price range and never bargain. Take it or leave it." It was a bargain at $600. I bought it and took it home.

(I read in the paper a few weeks later that my gun-dealer friend would be a "guest of the state" for a while. His specialty, as it turns out, was automatic weapons, which would explain his choice of store location.)

Thinking there may have been more to this bike than I knew, I ran a check of the serial number, and verified that the bike was a rare and very quick 1966 Triumph T-120 TT Special.

The TT was derived from the Triumph Bonneville street bike with modifications to the engine and the bike to make it suitable for racing. The target venues for the TT Special were (obviously) time trials, scrambles, desert races and flat track racing. The TT excelled in all these categories for many years.

The basic engine design placed the twin cams in the block, with pushrods activating the valves in the hemispherical combustion chambers. This gave the engine the breathing efficiency of dual overhead cams, but a very low center of gravity for excellent handling.

The TT Special engine was essentially the same design developed by Johnson Motors, the California dealer, for the Triumph streamliner that set a 230.3 mph two-way record at the Bonneville Salt Flats in 1962. The upgrades for the streamliner engine were 1 1/2 inch Amal GP carburetors (alcohol or gas, depending on jet size), 11:1 Robbins pistons, Jomo (Johnson Motors) full-race camshafts, larger valves and upgraded valve gear, and a fixed-advance magneto ignition.

Other standard modifications to the bike included elimination of the battery, battery box, headlight, taillight, center stand, mufflers, and all instrumentation except the tach. The bike had no ignition switch, just a kill button. Also added were aluminum fenders fore and aft, and the signature shorty pipes, which curved gracefully from the exhaust ports, tucked close together under the engine, and then splayed out to re-emerge just ahead of the rear wheel. The increased horsepower and reduced weight made the TT Special the quickest production bike in the country at the time, edging out even the Harley-Davidson Sportster.

On this particular TT, someone had mounted an aftermarket headlight and taillight and Bonneville street pipes, which is why I didn't identify it at first. But it was suitable for street use, which was my intended purpose. I replaced the dented tank and realigned the forks. It was ready to ride. And ride it I did.

The high compression ratio and fixed advance magneto requires that starting be a precise drill. Prod the starter to bring a piston up on the compression stroke. Then, launching from the footpegs, leap high into the air and come down full force on the kick start to spin the engine as quickly as possible. It's important to get this right the first time:

A timid kick results in the fixed-advance ignition spinning the engine backward. Then, the still-engaged kick starter kicks back, driving the rider's knee into his chest, and launching him over the handlebars.

Entertaining to watch, but painful for the participant.

On the Street

I left Pratt and Whitney to complete my PhD at UConn at Storrs. The TT Special was my daily transportation to and from school when the weather was good.

The countryside from Manchester to Storrs is filled with curvy, hilly, two-lane back roads—a motorcycle rider's dream. A straight shot to Storrs was 25 miles, but it often took me an hour or more to get there or back home. And I wasn't going 25 miles an hour. I arrived at work and home energized, to be sure.

One of my favorite stretches of road had a steep, sharp hill with a good landing zone on either side. On an evening ride with my bride, we hit the "wee-bump" at about 80 mph. She leaned back, pulling me back, which caused me to roll the throttle wide open. The front end came up and we cleared a good 80 feet in the air and landed in a perfect wheelie. When we got to school, she wanted to do it again on the way home. Meanwhile, I left to clean my shorts.

She was a great rider and a great sport. We could take the Interstate cloverleaf near our home at an angle sufficient enough to grind the side of her shoe off.

On the Track

Once on an afternoon ride, I took the TT to a practice flat track in the Glastonbury Mud Flats. As I leisurely circled the track on what appeared to be a street bike, the local champion on a 250 2-stroke dirt bike came out and challenged me.

We started half a lap apart. He had the weight advantage. But I had the power, the low center of gravity, and a bike created to rule the flat track.

Into the turns at 80 mph, flick the steering to get the rear end to come out, dial in the power, and turn the steering full reverse lock. Feet up all the way. Stable as a rock. Control the drift angle with the throttle. Then out of the corner and full throttle down the short straight. I passed him in two laps.

This bike was born to be king. And for a long time it was.

The End of the Road

I only had one accident. A Chevrolet Impala made an illegal left turn in front of me. Unable to stop I aimed for the center of his pre-guard-beam passenger door. I folded the door right into the front seat. The Triumph was unharmed. I was actually able to hold on, stay on the bike and keep it upright, though my arms and shoulders ached for a while.

I sold the TT Special after six years to a skinny young kid. I told him he was going to have to gain some weight if he wanted to start it. He didn't listen too well. He gave the kick start a timid prod and it launched him sideways off the bike. He sprained his ankle. Rather than being put off, he was excited about all the power. He had a big wad of cash—that kid paid me $850 so fast I barely saw him pull the roll of bills out of his pocket. Not one word of negotiation. I had to start it for him so he could ride it home.

The TT Special was in my care for five years. In all that time, and for all those swooping back roads and peg-dragging corners, it only needed one repair.

Purchased from a gun dealer at the end of a long, dirt road, Stenhouse's Triumph T-120 TT was a rare and powerful version of the Bonneville that was suitable for racing. It kept him entertained for five years, both on the street and on the track. *Mike Stenhouse*

Every time I see a Triumph, my mind goes back and I can't help grinning. The TT Special, with its minimalist competition look and sexy, down-swept pipes, is always the hit of any vintage motorcycle event.

And I am lucky enough to know why.

THE THOR IN THE MAPLE TREE

Collectors like to brag about the histories—the "provenance"—of their motorcycles. Some were owned by royalty or movie stars; others were used as engineering mules by their manufacturers. Mike Terry's 1911 Thor once belonged to a mature maple tree.

David White is a self-described picker from Lena, Illinois, who was searching a town in the northern part of his state for unwanted treasures in 2010 when he came across a collection of vintage bike parts with a twist worthy of Robert Ripley's *Believe It or Not!*

It was spring, but just barely. The woods were still nude and the snakes still hidden. White was in the area for an auction when he ran into a friend whose family farm went back three generations and was known to have a lot of scrap metal and antique farm machinery.

The original owner of the land had served in World War I—a remarkable claim for an area in which 60 native sons fought and only 16 returned. A hard post-war life taught the veteran to pinch a penny and never discard anything. His descendants continued the thrifty practice until well into the 21st century, and had just opened the property to junk men and scroungers when White arrived in town.

It was a bonanza for pickers.

"They never threw anything away," White said. "If something wasn't being used anymore, someone from the family hauled it into the woods and left it. There was an old Model T pickup, farm machinery, and tools everywhere. It was like a rusty museum of agriculture. I saw a century's worth of plows and farm implements, most of it in such bad shape it was only good for scrap."

White's first purchase was two boxes of Native American arrowheads, which he collected whenever possible. He offered $150, but the seller—his friend—thought that was too much and only took $100.

He went to a milk shed next, where he saw a pair of tractors that looked as if they had not been run in decades. "They were Case SCs, which J.I. Case made in Racine, Wisconsin, from 1940 to 1955," he said. "One had belonged to the grandpa; the other, the dad. He wanted $1,000 for the pair, which I gave him. Cases are not very collectible, so I ended up scrapping them. I probably paid too much."

The shed was full from top to bottom with machinery, including old binders, hayloaders, McCormick-Deering and Massey-Harris equipment, horse-drawn one- to six-bottom plows, and pull-type combines—the likes of which no one has used in 60 years. White bought it all.

White learned that two other junkers had already been over the property and had offered no money but said they would haul everything away for scrap,

This is the 1911 Thor frame and engine David White discovered while searching for old machines and scrap iron in Illinois. The single-cylinder engine was buried under a winter's worth of garbage in a barn, while the frame had been captured by a mature maple tree.

making White's cash on the barrelhead very attractive. He pulled out another $400 to claim all of the scrap iron that was scattered around the farm and in the woods. It would be hard work, but White's loader and torch would turn the big pieces into manageable chunks of profit.

He was looking around the inside of a shed as an old lady pulled bags of winter-stored trash out. Some boys from the family had already been combing the scrap and selling anything they could physically lift onto a trailer, but the trash had obscured a small single-cylinder engine marked "Thor" that was now visible to White. "I was buying some crock jars from the lady when I noticed the engine," he said. "All I had were $20 bills, and I was up to $50 worth of jars, so I said, 'How about we call it even at $60 if you throw in that little engine?'

"She agreed and said I could have the other motorcycle parts around back of the building for free. She told me one motorcycle had been leaning against a tree back there since before her father was born."

A day later, when White worked his way to the location of the free vintage motorcycles, he was not as happy as one might expect. "There were two motorcycle frames, although I didn't know what brand they were at the time," he said. "They were not just leaning against some trees; they had been absorbed into the body of a big maple and lifted off the ground during years of growth.

"One bike wasn't in there too bad. I was able to get it free just by cutting some branches. The other one was almost entirely encapsulated, though, and the swept-back handlebars were completely hidden by the trunk. It took me three days to get it free with my chainsaw. I went through a couple of blades getting it out, but the frame was intact and in good shape when I finally freed it."

White now had one Thor engine and two frames. He asked if anyone knew where the other engine was, and if there might be more motorcycles. "It turns out the other engine had been outside, so the kids grabbed it and scrapped it. They also found an Indian motorcycle, pried the emblem off as a keepsake, and sent the rest to the junkyard for crushing.

"The only reason I had an engine at all was because it was buried under trash, and the frames were saved because the tree was claiming them. I also found a Schwinn bicycle that the boys had missed." Scouring the grounds turned up a few Thor tools in a pouch, a sprocket, and a pedal assembly.

At home with his finds, White did some research on the Thor products. He found that the Thor Moto Cycle and Bicycle Co. was founded in Aurora, Illinois, in 1903 for the purpose of building parts for the growing motorcycle industry. Its parent, the Aurora Machine and Tool Co., was the main supplier of Indian parts in 1902. Thor primarily produced engines and frames for Indian, but the 1903 Thor catalog indicated it had every component needed to construct a motorcycle. By 1908, Indian had taken its foundry work in-house, and Thor was advertising complete motorcycles for sale through a dealer network.

The 1911 model engine White found marked the first Thor produced with a free-moving engine clutch on the single-cylinder bikes. Thor's end is a subject of some confusion, but it is safe to say the company stopped motorcycle production at some point during the years of 1918–1920.

"Thors weren't out for a long time," White said, "but they were part of that first Big Three, along with Indian and Harley. I didn't realize how historic they might be when I was cutting them out of the tree. Since they were built in Aurora, it looks like these two Thors got no more than an hour and a half away before the trees got them."

White could identify one of the frames as a Thor, but the other had no markings and was a mystery. "I put the engine and frames on eBay," he said. "Since I couldn't say for sure what it was, I just said the second frame was for 'an old motorcycle.'"

That's when collector Mike Terry of Toms River, New Jersey, first heard of White's discovery. "I was never really interested in Thors," Terry said. "I've had Flying Merkels, Popes, and Yales. I thought they were more interesting at the time."

His stable of 25 bikes includes some unusual barn finds, although he was not personally responsible for their discovery.

This 1911 Thor should look pretty good—in its lifetime, it traveled only an hour and a half from the Thor factory in Aurora, Illinois.

His 1913 Harley-Davidson twin was found disassembled in a collapsed building by a great-nephew of the property's owner. He had been cleaning up the wood to resell it when he found the engine and what he thought was a bicycle frame. Figuring anything that old with the name Harley-Davidson stamped on it was worth some good money, he posted it on Craigslist, where it was bought by Terry's friend Todd Bertrang, whom Terry describes as "a motorcycle guru who has had a lot of great bikes in the last 30 years." Terry traded Bertrang a '54 Harley Panhead with original paint for the '13 basket case.

Terry's 1913 Harley single-cylinder bike was found in a porch in Iowa in 2011. Terry thinks the bike lay on its side for years, because water got into the engine, and one side of the cylinder was very rusty. The owner, whose family had it in the porch, bought it used in 1920, an event that was captured in an old photo.

Terry's 1914 Henderson was missing its engine when it was found in a landfill in Wyoming on a 20,000-acre estate. A tractor had run over it, but after he acquired it around 1995 (in exchange for a '47 Harley springer front fork), Terry had a fabricator straighten the tubes. It has since been restored.

Terry knew a lot about bikes from that era, but had no idea what bid to place on David White's Thor lots on eBay. "I saw the Thor engine was up to

A close-up shows that the metal of this 1913 Thor frame did not fare so well buried in the tree. The handlebars and support tube were quite chewed up.

$500 already," Terry said. "I just figured out how bad I wanted everything and made my bids. I won all three, but I was surprised that the unmarked frame went for as high as it did."

White gave Terry a bonus for buying all three lots—two of the Thor wrenches he discovered near the bikes.

After receiving and investigating his wins, Terry verified that the engine and the frame that had been freed from the tree were from 1911. The second, unidentified frame was either a 1913 or 1914 model—the two years were identical. One Thor enthusiast told Terry it was definitely a '14 because of the way the handlebars are bent.

Terry has developed a fascination with Thors, and plans to do more research on the subject. He recently bought two Thor engines, a 1914 twin and a 1913 single, for his barn-find projects. "I'll probably install the single into the tree frame," he said, "because I like the way the singles drive."

As for White, the picker has expanded his scope of items to look for at estate sales and in old barns. "I've found some old motorcycles in the past, but didn't really know what they were worth," he said. "Those Thors really opened my eyes. I've seen frames go through auction that brought $160 or $200. Looking back, I probably should have bought them."

WORD OF MOUTH

Sure, watching for ads in the local newspaper or scanning eBay and Craigslist on a daily basis will occasionally turn up a diamond, but most successful barn-finders will tell you that the best method for hunting down buried treasure is to hear about it from someone else.

Why? Because by the time the ad hits eBay or the paper, thousands of folks are seeing the same ad at the same time. So if 1,000 collectors are looking at the ad, you have a 1 in 1,000 chance of owning the bike of your dreams. Better to be the sole person to hear about that bike from a neighbor, friend, or co-worker of the owner. Then your chances are 1 in 1!

California's Mark Mitchell and his friend Mike Long have searched out quite a few interesting cars and bikes.

A few years ago, Long went to look at a 1958 Mercedes that was for sale. He decided not to purchase the car, but before he left, he asked the seller—a man named Dennis—whether he knew of any other interesting cars in the area.

"No, I don't know of any car," Dennis told Long. "But I do know of a fantastic collection of motorcycles."

Dennis went on to explain that a close friend's father assembled the collection before passing away about 12 years earlier. After the funeral, Dennis helped the widow move the motorcycles and parts from a corrugated tin shed into a drier and more secure semi-truck container.

Over the years, collectors would occasionally approach the widow in an effort to purchase one or two of the more desirable bikes, but she had no desire to break up the collection her husband so passionately assembled.

When Long came back home from the Mercedes trip, he immediately called Mark, knowing his friend's inability to pass up a good barn-find adventure.

"He asked if I'd like to go see the bikes and try to negotiate a purchase with the widow," said Mitchell. They drove to the woman's house in a nice, rural neighborhood. She gave them permission to inspect the bikes.

"When the doors of the storage container were opened, I was overwhelmed," said Mitchell. "To see all those bikes covered in dust was an incredible sight."

But the fact that the bikes were packed so tightly made it difficult to identify more than the few closest to the door.

The two barn-finders, Mitchell and Long, had heard through the grapevine that there was at least one Vincent and one Indian, but other than that, they could only see a number of Triumphs fading back into the darkness of the storage container.

The other bike Mitchell kept for himself was this 1951 Vincent Rapide. *Mark Mitchell*

They discussed the best method to place a fair value on the entire collection. They tried to come up with a value for each bike, but that proved too difficult because they simply could not get to the back of the container to inspect the inventory. They finally settled on some values for the three of the more collectible bikes they could see: the Vincent, which was a 1951 Rapide; the 1948 Indian Bonneville Chief; and a 1950 Triumph Thunderbird. They simply applied an average price to the remaining bikes.

Then there was the barn, which was loaded with motorcycle parts—mostly gas tanks, wheels, engines, transmissions, carburetors, fenders, and seats. They determined a final value on the bikes and went into the house to negotiate with the widow. For her, it was an emotional process, but she finally settled and agreed to part with her late husband's treasures.

"We told her we would move out everything and leave her storage area swept clean," said Mitchell.

Mitchell wanted to start removing bikes immediately, but, alas, his truck only had enough room for one bike. So he brought home the Indian, which he was too excited about to leave behind.

When they returned to remove the entire inventory, they were ready: they had rented the largest U-Haul box truck they could find—26 feet—as well as two full-size pickup trucks with trailers. It was an even bigger bonanza than they had thought.

Mitchell had his eyes on just 2 of the 16 bikes in the collection. One was this unrestored 1948 Indian Chief, which he retained for himself. *Mark Mitchell*

"We had eight people to help us load," Mitchell said. And it still took four hours to hustle the inventory from the trailer and the barn into the trucks in the hot midday sun. "Then there was the four-hour drive home . . . we were exhausted by the end."

Once they arrived at Mitchell's shop in Ventura, they started to make a plan to dispose of their booty. Besides the Vincent, Indian, and Triumph T'bird, the stash included a 1969 BSA Victor Special, a 1983 Harley-Davidson Sportster, and 13 additional Triumphs.

"The original idea was to sell everything and simply make a profit," Mitchell said. "But how often are you able to find a Vincent in a barn? That's the sort of thing people write books about. We were both quite attached to the bikes, but realized we needed to let them go."

Mitchell wanted to keep the Vincent and maybe the Indian, and Long had fallen in love with the Triumph Thunderbird, so they made an agreement between the two of them to keep those three and sell the rest. "We cleaned up the remaining 15 bikes and offered them for sale," Mitchell said. "We had originally thought of selling the bikes one-by-one, which would have yielded us more money, but decided to sell the entire lot to one collector in Australia. I don't regret selling the rest of the bikes to one collector. It was easier, and once you find a Vincent, everything else doesn't mean quite as much."

Quite a treasure trove: Mike Long (left) and barn-finding buddy Mark Mitchell became the lucky owners of this motorcycle collection, which had been kept in a storage container since the original central California owner died. *Mark Mitchell*

Mitchell said that the three bikes he and Long kept will not be restored, but instead cleaned up just enough without removing the patina. "As the years go on, nice original bikes like these will be much more difficult to find than totally restored ones," he said.

Some People Have All The Luck...

Just one week later, Mitchell was on to another discovery. He said, "I heard from a friend about a bankruptcy auction that offered a few classic cars and motorcycles.

"He was able to buy one of the cars, and I successfully bid on two motorcycles—a 1959 Velocette 500 Venom and a 1974 Norton 850 Commando. Both these bikes were in great shape and would have been 'keepers' if I hadn't just [blown] my entire savings on the Vincent and the Indian a week earlier. It's amazing what's still out there and waiting to be found!"

And word-of-mouth is the best way, it seems, to find it.

INVENTORY OF MARK MITCHELL'S
AND MIKE LONG'S DISCOVERIES:

1951 Vincent Rapide 1000

1948 Indian Bonneville Chief

1969 BSA 441 Victor Special

1983 Harley-Davidson Sportster Roadster

1950 Triumph Thunderbird

1963 Triumph T120 Bonneville 650

1965 Triumph T120R Bonneville 650

1966 Triumph TT100 500

1968 Triumph T120R Bonneville 650

1969 Triumph T100R 500

1970 Triumph T120R Bonneville 650 (3)

1970 Triumph T100C 500

1970 Triumph TR6C 650

1973 Triumph TR5 Trophy Trail 500

1977 Triumph T140 750

1983 Triumph T140 TSS 750 Electro (with Westlake eight-port head)

ONE TZ SUMMER
by Richard Pollock

Richard Pollock is the owner of Mule Motorcycles, a one-man operation in Poway, California. He has built more than 110 bikes for customers around the world and has quite a few barn finds to share.

In 1979, one person bought four of the world's most expensive, fastest race bikes in crates as an investment and left them in storage for the rest of his life. The story of how I found three of those Yamaha TZ750 road racers 12 years later and accidentally jumpstarted the market for TZs is a convoluted tale that could only happen in southern California.

I've been into motorcycles since 1969, and I've competed in motocross, flat track, and road racing. When I moved to San Diego in 1975, I started working in motorcycle shops and wound up at a Yamaha dealership owned by Paul Dahmen, where riders such as Dave Aldana competed on our bikes, including, as of its introduction in 1975, Yamaha's TZ750.

The TZ750 was the IndyCar of motorcycles. It was a production road-racing bike, hand-assembled at the factory, but without lights, generator, side stand, or turn signals. Yamaha had been making 125s, 250s, 350s, and 500s for competition, but nobody saw the TZ750 coming.

The engine was a pair of 350cc top ends mounted to a common lower end with reed-valve induction, four exhaust pipes, and 130 horsepower. It reminded me of a Vincent, which was nothing more than a motor with some accessories attached; the TZ worked off that same philosophy, and its top speed was around 190 miles per hour.

The TZ750 was a huge breakthrough for the sport of motorcycle racing. Before it came out, teams pushed street engines beyond their limits on the track, but the TZ could go half a season without the crew taking the top end off. It was so tractable and forgiving that it turned decent riders into front runners. At the 1979 Daytona races, two-thirds of the field ran TZ750s

Everybody who was winning at the time had them, such as Kenny Roberts, Steve Baker, Gene Romero, and Freddie Spencer. Jay Springsteen was a Harley-Davidson factory rider—he rode Harleys on the dirt courses—and even he did time on a Yamaha TZ.

They were so crazy exotic and expensive that rarity was guaranteed. There were two shops in San Diego County that sold them—Don Vesco Yamaha, and our place, Kearny Mesa Yamaha. Kearny Mesa sold about three TZs a year during their heyday; legend has it only 200 were produced worldwide.

My First TZ750

In 1984, I thought I would make a little money with a TZ rebuild project. One of the guys who raced out of our shop and a friend of his bought a TZ to start their own team. They went to all the nationals that year, but at Laguna Seca the rider crashed, breaking his lower leg and hurting his knee.

The bike was a complete wreck, but I traded a car for the TZ's remains and restored it. I got a straight frame from former Triumph race bike fabricator Rob North, bought new wheels, and picked up some fresh brake rotors. By the time I finished it off with a custom paint job, I had $4,000 in it and figured to make a couple of grand off of selling it.

It went on the market right before Daytona, which I thought would be a perfect time to buy a race-ready TZ. Unfortunately, I had misread the market for a bike that was, at the time, nine years old, so my *Cycle News* ad only brought me enough money to break even.

I got out of the TZ business but returned with great enthusiasm and a tremendous amount of luck seven years later.

The First "TZ Summer" Bike

I left my service manager job with Kearny Mesa in 1988, but I visited the shop often to buy parts and visit my buddies. One day in 1991, I was talking to one of the salesmen, who told me a young kid had come in saying he was taking bids on a motorcycle he had for sale, sort of like a silent auction.

"What kind of bike?" I asked the salesman.

"When I tell you," he said, "you'll mortgage your house to get it."

I laughed and said, "There's no bike like that out there."

"It's a TZ750." He paused. "In the crate."

That made my ears perk up because the sting of my earlier TZ disappointment had faded, and I still, darn it, had a soft spot for the beautiful but obsolete world-beater. I called the kid and asked for more information about the bike he was selling. He told me an incredible story that made me shake my head in wonder at how some people's brains work.

In 1979, his father's accountant said he needed to "divest some funds" or pay more in taxes, so he went to a Yamaha shop in Escondido and asked to see the most expensive bike he could buy. They told him he could ride home on a top-of-the-line XS 1100 touring bike for a mere $3,800. When that didn't satisfy him, the salesman said, "Or we could order a TZ750 for $10,000."

The father said, "I'll take four."

When the four crated race bikes arrived, the dealership "serviced out" (prepped for riding, but, not street legal) one of the TZs as instructed, and loaded the others on a delivery truck. The dad rode the uncrated bike home, at night, with the truck following him with its high beams on. All of the bikes were placed in the garage of a huge house in the hyper-expensive Rancho Sante Fe neighborhood—and basically forgotten by all involved for 11 years.

The kid said his father committed suicide and it was up to him to sell off his belongings. In the six months since his father's passing, two of the crate bikes and the uncrated bike had disappeared to support, the kid suspected, his brother's drug habits.

It didn't sound as if the seller knew much about the TZ, its history, or its value, so I thought my chances of getting it were good. I used a very weird logic to calculate the bid:

The bike retailed for around $10,000 when new, which meant the dealer cost was probably in the $6,000 range. It had never been ridden, so nothing on it was broken—which was important because obsolete race bikes don't have what you would call a "parts network," especially once they fall out of use.

Here is the first bike of the TZ Summer bunch, stripped to the frame and freshly powder-coated. Owner Richard Pollock also had the hardware cadmium plated before the rebuild.

76

I figured I could not lose money at $6,000, so that's what I offered, even though I would have to get a quick loan to cover it.

When the kid accepted my bid, he told me there was just one small problem. He had opened the crate to get the bike out and found that a squirrel had made a nest and peed all over the swingarm and some other parts. Those pinewood plank crates were never intended for long-term storage; they were used to keep the cargo upright and protected during a ship voyage. There wasn't even a plastic bag over the Yamaha, just some cables holding it in place.

The rodent news did not deter me, and I felt it might actually give me some bargaining leverage, so I drove to the address and pulled up in front of a house so big it had an eight-stall barn garage. The TZ was in the family room, leaning against a pool table.

On the pool table were two large cardboard boxes. Those boxes held the unbelievably valuable spares kit, which included 10 sets of rings, 10 pistons, two crankshafts, two cylinders, two clutches, intake manifolds, exhaust gaskets, umpteen sparkplugs, a stack of sprockets, and clutch springs. This is what a vintage race-bike expert would call "hitting the jackpot."

The Yamaha did not look bad at all—just a little crusty in the back half. We negotiated the price down to $5,000, in light of the squirrel problem. I probably could have taken the bike for as little as $2,000—the kid had no idea what he had—but I was so blown away by what I was seeing that my bargaining skills were not very sharp.

I got the bike home and started working on it as quickly as possible, my intent being to fix the problem areas and sell it for a nice profit. That might sound very unromantic coming from someone who builds, fixes, and enjoys bikes, but the truth of the matter is that I like to build them more than I like to own them. I'm not a collector.

I put 20 hours of easy work into the TZ's rehabilitation. I took it apart, powdercoated the frame, rebuilt the swingarm bushing, replaced the rear wheel's spokes, sanded and repainted the exhaust pipes, got some bolts cadmium plated, bead blasted the fork sliders and triple clamps, and put it all back together.

My classified ad in *Cycle News* asked for $15,000, but I really wasn't sure what the market would bear. A buyer for the Barber Vintage Motorsports Museum called and was very interested, but kept insisting that there should be a fairing with the TZ. I could not convince him that Yamaha never sold its TZs with fairings—the reality is, teams individually created or bought the fairings because everyone had different ideas about how the aerodynamics should work. I had personally unpacked many TZs from crates while working for Kearny Mesa, and not one bike came with a fairing. Our disagreement over this issue killed the deal, but I was pleased to notice that some TZs eventually made it into the museum and are displayed just as they were delivered to dealers—without fairings.

Later, I received a call from Dale Newton, who owned Aero Union in Chico, California. His company converted World War II bombers into firefighting apparatus, and he had quite a collection of motorcycles. He drove his van 600 miles to look at the Yamaha and the spares kit and offered me a firm $13,500.

I told him, "If you give me $15,000, I'll feed you lunch and throw in this framed factory promotional poster of the TZ750."

He said, "I'm willing to pay $13,500."

My wife made lunch, and we ate while I thought about it. Considering how little I had in the bike, more than doubling my money seemed like an attractive proposition, so I agreed and the TZ went to its new home up north—without the framed poster. Dale was so confident I would take his price that he had a cashier's check already made out for the amount.

I later visited Dale and saw his collection. When I called a few years after that to arrange another visit, I learned he had passed away. His son sold the company to new owners who one day opened a large shipping container in one of the hangars and discovered it was packed full of exotic motorcycles, and even had an original Cobra. That's what a marketing expert would call "added value."

The Second "TZ Summer" Bike

Shortly after I cleared $8,500 for a couple of weeks of work with the first TZ, a friend at a Yamaha shop in Escondido said another kid was trying to sell another '79 TZ750. I thought this had to be an amazing coincidence, a sign from the universe—or one of the four Rancho Santa Fe motorcycles.

He was asking $2,000, which suggested to me it was no longer in the crate, but I had to investigate. I got $2,000 out of the bank and pulled my bike trailer to the address, where this young kid showed me the bike in the old garage.

There was only one problem. Someone had ridden the bike with the bulletproof engine so inexpertly that he managed to throw a rod and crack the crankcase. That took some skill.

He lowered the asking price to $800 and told me that a friend of his had a couple of spares kits and could sell me all the parts I needed to fix it. This news made me wonder if that friend also had one of the Rancho Santa Fe TZs.

I paid him the $800, wrote down the address of the friend with spare parts, and toted the broken Yamaha back to my garage.

With its tank out of the way, here is a clear view of bike number two's four carburetors and monoshock suspension.

The Third "TZ Summer" Bike

A few days later, I found myself in a truck parking lot out in the middle of nowhere, looking for TZ number three. When I say this was a "shady" place, I don't mean it was a cool spot to get away from the heat; I mean it looked like the Manson family compound. It was a little creepy.

At the back of the property was a clearing with a metal container shed and a mobile home that must have been for a night watchman at one time.

I knew I was at the right place, because when I pulled up, the guy I was there to meet was doing donuts in an old Camaro in the yard, while a few of his friends stood on the sidelines. Judging from their crazy eyes and amped-up energy, he and his buddies were—for lack of a more precise description—wired.

When I could get the owner's attention, I cautiously said I would like to buy some TZ parts and that his friend had sent me. He led me to a storage shed. In the shed was a '79 TZ750—almost certainly the third of the Rancho Sante Fe bunch—leaning against a bench. I could see it was all stock, but the gas tank had been stripped of its paint, and there was a scuff on it.

For $200, I bought a pair of crankshafts and a bunch of other parts—almost a full spares kit. Trying to sound as casual as possible, I asked if he would be interested in selling the TZ. He told me to come back the next day and he would think about it.

The third TZ750 is going back together in this photo. Pollock polished the rims and gave a gold anodizing treatment to the sprocket with his final TZ. Pollock also polished the front fork sliders, triple clamps, and rims. It makes for a more attractive finish, but he now thinks he should have kept it stock.

I returned the next day, this time with $2,000 in cash and a shotgun in the truck. Unfortunately, the TZ owner had had a bad night and was in a manic mood; he told me to go away.

I left and turned my focus back to bike number two of the bunch, got it ready for sale, and made a $6,000 profit. Now I was really motivated to pursue that third TZ. Considering the owner's unconventional lifestyle, I knew the guy would need cash soon, so I paid him another visit.

Back at the truck park, I found he was in a relatively stable mood, but I was still anxious about being there. About the bike, he asked, "What'll you give me for it?"

I said, "I'll give you 'two' for it."

His eyes lit up with what I assumed was enthusiasm. "You'll give me two *hundred* for the bike?"

My nervousness over the situation must have overloaded my brain once again, because my response flew out before I had a chance to think it over.

"No, I'll give you two *thousand* dollars for it."

As the words were leaving my lips, I realized I had just made a large mistake.

"Hell yeah!" he said.

After I got the third bike back to my shop, I had Rob North work his magic on the gas tank, which looked like new on its return. The rest of the TZ cleaned up well. I combined the third TZ, all the spares I had, and the chassis of a TZ 700 (the early iteration of the 750 model) and sold the whole package to a collector in Los Angeles.

This is the bike that started the crazy TZ Summer for Richard Pollock, exactly as it appeared after being pulled from its crate after 12 years of storage. Notice the surface rust on the chain and exhaust pipe. This angle shows the TZ750's race-style gas tank, which features a hold-down clamp on the rear. This system gives easy access to the engine but has been known to let the tank fly free during a crash.

Out of the Market Again

The funny thing about that period in 1991 that I call "TZ Summer" is that my three bikes selling for prices no one had ever paid before may have possibly pushed up the value of *all* TZ750s. Today, you can't touch one for less than $20,000, and good ones bring more than $25,000.

I like to think I had something to do with making these fantastic, historic bikes popular again.

BIKE IN THE BASEMENT
by Larry Edsall

When Mark Johnson first heard the stories about an old guy in town who had World War II–era Harley-Davidson motorcycles still in their original crates, he was a high school student in East Hanover, New Jersey, in the middle of the 1960s.

Like so many other students of his generation, Johnson moved away after graduation. He went to college. He taught high school. He got into the printing business. He ran printing companies and then managed sales for a printing company so large it was among the Fortune 500. He traveled the world.

And then one day he hung up his suits and returned to his roots. He opened his own motorcycle shop (Custom Bike Works), which soon expanded with a specialized powdercoating business (Mac Coatings) and a custom bike-building business (The Big Johnson Motorcycle Co.). Johnson set up his shops in Dover, New Jersey, less than 20 miles from where he'd grown up.

In 2010, Johnson ran into an old high school buddy who mentioned that the old guy with the motorcycles in crates had died. The friend thought the old bikes were still intact, and suggested Johnson investigate on behalf of his motorcycle business.

Johnson did. He tracked down a phone number, supposedly for the old guy with the bikes, and called it. Turns out the old guy wasn't dead. He answered the telephone. He even invited Johnson over to his house.

"I have Mondays off [from the bike shop] to do my errands," Johnson said. Monday after Monday, week after week, month after month, Johnson would call and visit Thomas Iradi, who said that, indeed, he had several WWII-vintage Harleys in his house—in his basement, to be precise. But through all those Mondays, those weeks and those months, Iradi wouldn't let Johnson see the bikes.

"He's a really neat old guy who can be a real pain in the ass, and I tell him that all the time," Johnson said of Iradi, who had been a motorcycle mechanic and later a motorcycle messenger during World War II.

Instead of exploring the bikes in Iradi's basement, Johnson (who says patience is not among his virtues) had to be content to simply sit and listen to a couple hours of Iradi's storytelling, often in the company of Iradi's younger brother, Jimmy. They were tales of youthful adventures, of war stories, of motorcycle rides, stories that changed from week to week, to the point Johnson wasn't sure how valid any of them might truly be.

"But every Monday for nine months, I spent the afternoon with these two guys and he finally let me go down into the basement and take pictures," Johnson said. "Oh my God!"

Wheelchair user Thomas Iradi hadn't been in his own basement in some two decades until Mark Johnson finally convinced him to let Johnson see the trove of World War II–era Harleys.

Johnson insisted Thomas Iradi go to the basement with him—no small feat since Iradi's legs had been amputated, leaving Iradi a wheelchair user. Iradi also was nearly blind. "He was losing his eyesight," Johnson said, "but none of his spunk!

"He hadn't been down into his basement in nearly 30 years," Johnson said. "I'd given him, as he said, an opportunity to go back down and 'see' the bikes with his own hands."

What Iradi saw with his hands and Johnson with his eyes was, in Johnson's words, "shocking."

"There were nine WLAs, all '42s except for one '41, and there were five civilian WLs, ranging from 1938 to 1949, along with shelves and shelves of parts. Everything was Flatheads. Everything was 45s."

Obviously, Johnson wanted to buy a bike. Iradi was reluctant.

"I had to wrestle to get him to let me buy something," Johnson said. "He finally sold me a 1949, which was the newest bike Iradi had—and which he liked the least." Johnson planned to use his purchase as his entry into Harleys of the era and to find his way to those who knew about such bikes and the parts to restore and maintain them.

Seeing Johnson's sincerity, Iradi finally agreed to let Johnson advertise one of his bikes for sale on eBay.

Vintage Harleys, both military and civilian versions, had been sitting in Thomas Iradi's basement for decades. The bikes were high and dry when Hurricane Irene flooded his basement in the summer of 2011.

Vintage Harley-Davidson parts, pieces, and even engines were found in Tom's basement, some in their original containers.

An original V-twin engine—a little worse-for-wear after several decades, but ready for restoration.

"It got tremendous interest. We were flabbergasted at how many people were emailing me," Johnson said. "I didn't leave it on the site that long because there were questions about the title. But I was able to put a list together of people with an interest." Johnson was able to sort through the issues with the bike's title and sold the bike to someone in Australia.

As soon as he handed the cash to Irani, "he asked if I wanted to sell another one." It didn't take long for Johnson not only to sell another one, but four more of the WLA Harleys.

Disaster struck, however, in the form of Hurricane Irene.

In late August 2011, Irene worked her way up across the Caribbean and up the East Coast. She killed nearly 60 people and accounted for more than $10 billion in property losses. East Hanover is located at the convergence of the Passaic and Whippany rivers. Irani's house is in the Whippany's flood plain. "There was three and a half feet of water in his basement," Johnson discovered.

Fortunately, three of the bikes had been stored atop work benches and only parts of their wheels had been in the water. Johnson was able to remove everything from the basement, sold the bikes that had suffered flood damage, cleaned all the parts, and has been cataloging them for sale.

As you might expect, Irani himself is undaunted.

"He's started a new adventure," Johnson said, explaining that Irani is having Johnson restore the three remaining, to get them running so Irani can give them to his grandchildren.

"The neat thing is, this guy is for real," Johnson said. "He was a World War II motorcycle mechanic and then he became a messenger in the war. He worked on the bikes and he rode them in the war.

"And they've really changed the whole personality of my shop," Johnson added, explaining that he now has a '47 Knucklehead being fixed next to a '52, next to a brand-new Harley undergoing customization. "I've met some of the old players and have found new sources."

Johnson has kept two of the bikes in the basement. The '49 that he first bought from Irani, and a '42 WLA "that I'm going to try to put back the way it was."

CHAPTER THREE

Real Character

SOUTHERN HOSPITALITY
by Somer Hooker

Those familiar with Tennessee know that the upper east side of the state has always been a bit different from the rest of it. After being discharged from the Navy, I wound up moving to Knoxville. Due to my interest in vintage motorcycles I soon learned about Dobie Reed. Dobie had a shop made up of several buildings on a hillside in Del Rio. It was the last stop when leaving Newport and heading to North Carolina on Highway 41. Highway 41 was the major highway to North Carolina prior to I-40 being carved out of the Smoky Mountains in the 1970s. Dobie had been a franchised Indian and BMW dealer (the showroom had a dirt floor!). In the back of *Cycle Magazine* in the 1950s, Dobie ran an ad stating "All motorcyclists welcome."

In the mid-1980s, my brother and I drove up there to visit. Dobie was courteous enough. He let us peek through windows and see what we could see. Dobie wasn't too eager to allow access, though. I do remember seeing a crated BMW Steib sidecar sitting in one of the buildings. He would not discuss selling it. We were cordial and bid him good day.

Dobie's shop was on a loop that I loved to ride. It took me through the mountains of eastern Tennessee and western North Carolina. It was always fun to stop and talk with Dobie.

I learned that you didn't try to engage him at noon on Saturdays. That was when wrestling came on TV. Once, I lingered a moment too long and he literally ran up the side of the mountain to get to his TV. Dobie was in his sixties then!

Finally one time he let me into his shop. The BMW sidecar was gone. He said he had been offered a lot of money for it and sold it. I looked all around the room at the derelict Indians and Harleys. From the joists hung hundreds of gas tanks and fenders from American motorcycles. A battered BMW R-51/2 leaned against the wall; one cylinder had been knocked off in an accident. Because of the BMW's pressed crankshaft arrangement this pretty much ensured the requirement of a teardown. "I'm going to try to heat it up and twist it [a connecting rod] straight," Dobie noted. My head was still swimming at the array of iron in the building, some of it dating back to the 1920s. Nothing was for sale.

Later, I was invited to his house for coffee. Like Dobie, his wife was pleasant and always easy to chat with. We all sat and made small talk in a room with a dirt floor (this is eastern Tennessee, after all).

One day my wife and I rode up on my Vincent Rapide. I figured this would be a good ice breaker. He admired my bike and then told me about having a Rapide. "I bought it at Daytona. It was on the Indian stand." (Indian

When enthusiast Somer Hooker first met hoarder Dobie Reed, this is the scene he stumbled across. Dobie had been an Indian and BMW dealer in the 1950s, and owned a huge stash of bikes and parts, but seldom sold anything. Here he is posed with his granddaughter. *Somer Hooker*

distributed Vincent in the early 1950s). "A bunch of locals had heard of it and came down and wanted to race me, and I told them to hold on as I needed to warm it up." Dobie said he chugged down the road a bit and then came flying back by his shop doing over 100 mph. When he returned, he said, "Well now, it's warmed up!" His challengers offered nothing but excuses: *I gotta get home . . . my wife is expecting me . . .*

Later, Dobie sold the bike to Vincent dealer Gene Aucott in Philadelphia. Aucott remembered his trip down there. "It was a show-model Rapide," he said. "Everything had been chromed instead of cadmium plated." They laid it down on the back of Gene's station wagon and brought it back.

The late George Leo once reminiced about being at a bike convention in the area, and bumping into Dobie. Most of east Tennessee was dry back then, and Leo was curious as to where he might get a drink. Dobie denied knowing anything about any moonshine in the area, but stated that if he wanted to buy an old panel truck, they just might find some in it. They bought the truck, and found the moonshine.

This had been Reed's dirt-floor showroom, located in eastern Tennessee. Reed was well known among motorcycle collectors. *Somer Hooker*

The collection of motorcycles stashed outside Dobie's shop grew and grew. Folks said he did repairs for locals and then put liens on vehicles if they couldn't pay. He covered them with old shower curtains, tarps, and whatnot. It slowly became a hoarder's domain.

I once noticed some Indians leaning against the back of a shed. They were slowly rusting as their tires deflated and lowered their mass to the ground. I stopped by periodically on an old bike to visit. He'd always ask, "Checking to see if I'm still alive? Longevity runs in my family."

Later, work took me away from east Tennessee. I went into business for myself in the motorcycle trade and stopped by to visit Dobie from time to time. In 1992, I was en route to North Carolina and decided to visit Dobie. It was a nice spring day, and he came out to look at my trailer and we talked. I asked about looking in his shop. "I can't get the door open," he answered. It was blocked—Dobie had been buying lawn mower engines for a dollar "for the hardware." He used to open the door and throw them in. After a while, the mound got so big that they rolled back down and blocked the door from opening. He couldn't get in his own shop!

As we walked around back I surveyed the rusting Indian Four and Chief frames. They had frost blowout. This occurs when the moisture that humidity has formed in metal frames freezes and expands, causing the tubing to explode. Suddenly, I could feel something snap in me. I confronted him. "Look here, Dobie, this frame is ruined! No one can ever use this. It is no good to anyone now!" I all but rubbed his nose in it. He mumbled unintelligibly and I wandered out to my van and said goodbye.

Years later I was traveling with John Parham of J&P fame and founder of the National Motorcycle Museum in Anamosa, Iowa. We had been to the Barber Museum in Birmingham and then driven over to Dale Walksler's Wheels Through Time Museum in North Carolina. We stopped for gas in Newport, Tennessee. I told John, "Hey, there used to be an old guy up the road 14 miles and he had a lot of old bikes. Let's drive down there."

When we pulled up, there was a semi-trailer parked in front. Parts and bikes were piled in. Two women and a man were there and eyed me suspiciously. As I approached them, they asked what I wanted. I inquired about Dobie and was informed that he had died. I immediately began letting them know I had known him and started telling them details that proved a relationship going back awhile. I learned the man was Dobie's son, and he relaxed, though the women still eyed us suspiciously. I walked into what had been his show room. In the display case were Buco hats and jackets from the 1950s. The counter had been an old Matchless crate. On the wall were stapled old pictures of riders in biker hats astride BMW singles. I had a camera in my pocket and started to pull it out. "No pictures," his daughter informed me. I slipped it back in my pocket and looked around. Convinced she had wandered off, I pulled it out again. "No pictures, I told you!" Busted again. I stared in disbelief at four or five original paint fenders that had been stacked one atop another. We watched as a gas tank was casually hurled up into the back of the truck. "This is our third truck load," they said.

The family was convinced that the parts were in danger here. They were sure that some of the bikes had already been stolen. I don't think many of them had had too much contact with Dobie. We inquired what they were going to do with the stuff. "Thinking of opening a museum," was the reply. Then another car pulled up and another woman got out. It was the third sister. We were told it was time to go.

I learned that one person bought up all of the American bikes. Dobie's son and the others discovered that what they had wasn't as valuable as they thought. This was my first exposure to a hoarder. It wouldn't be my last, but I realized that some people just "love 'em to death."

THE FREE KIWI TRIUMPH
by Brad Bowling

Finding undervalued automotive treasures in unlikely places was easier in the 1950s, when 40-year-old vehicles were considered junk that survived World War II's scrap-metal drives.

Today, the Internet and televised events, such as Barrett-Jackson's annual Scottsdale auctions, have given every farmer with a stripped Chevrolet or Norton frame in his barn the idea he's sitting on a goldmine.

Brian Rankine has lived in New Zealand's city of Palmerston North on the North Island for all of his 75 years. After more than a half-century of knocking on strange doors and peeking into decrepit storage buildings, Rankine has amassed a collection of 60 classic cars, trucks, motorcycles, tractors, and steam-powered boats—many of which he bought for only a few pounds or took home for free.

His acquisition of a 1913 Triumph Model C motorcycle in 1957 is typical of the stories we often hear from the golden age of barn finds.

"I was in a secondhand car parts shop in my town," Rankine recalled, "when the subject of old cars came up. One guy said he knew of a coal delivery man who had seen a veteran [vintage] car in a shed but wasn't interested in it."

Rankine had followed such slender threads before to find desirable old vehicles, so he called the delivery man, who shared the location with him. The address happened to be smack in the middle of his hometown.

"The old lady who lived there had been a widow for a long time," Rankine said. "Her late husband was a dentist who had traveled a lot outside the country, going on safaris in Africa and other adventures. Their house was full of wild animal trophies. He fought in World War I, came back safely in 1918, then died a year later from the flu.

"She took me to a lean-to shed on her property. The car turned out to be an American-made 1910 Flanders that was mostly complete, except that its back end was on blocks because someone had removed the rear axle. It had been parked for 40 years, since her husband's death. She told me someone had come along in the 1920s, asking to pull some parts off of the Flanders, and might have left some pieces in the chicken coop."

Buried in the dirt in the chicken coop run was the Flanders' axle, minus the pinion gear. Rankine and the car's owner agreed on a nominal price— just a few dollars—and she suggested he investigate a room behind the shed for more parts.

"Her late husband was a gun enthusiast, so his workshop had a lot of tools and metal-working machines. In the middle of the shop, I saw a pre–World War I 550cc Triumph motorcycle. The dentist had bought it

Brian Rankine has owned this Triumph Model C for over 55 years. "The engine turns over," he says, "and, in true Triumph tradition, it still leaks oil on the ground." This photograph was taken in 2011, although nothing has changed about the Triumph Model C since 1957 when he discovered it in a gun workshop behind a shed in Palmerston North, New Zealand. *Gytha Riddell*

new, ridden it a few years, then parked it when he went off to war. It had been sitting untouched in his dark gun room for four decades and was in great shape.

"When I asked the lady about the Triumph, she said I could take it with the car!"

Modern readers are probably shocked at the thought of valuable collector vehicles being given away like so much scrap, but this practice was typical in the years before enthusiasts began restoring them in huge numbers. Around the world, the handcrafted cars and motorcycles of the Veteran, Brass, and Vintage eras were considered obsolete relics from the late 1940s through the early 1970s—more trouble than they were worth to keep running. Barn finders such as Rankine learned that a little polite conversation was often all it took to purchase one of these desirable classics; they used that period to drag home every unloved vehicle they could find.

Did the widow have mixed feelings about parting with the Flanders and Triumph? Probably. Although they carried happy memories of her departed

The 1913 Triumph Model C was acquired as an accessory to this 1910 American-made Flanders automobile. *Gytha Riddell*

husband's short time as their owner, they also reminded her of New Zealand's grimmest and darkest years. More than 18,000 New Zealanders died fighting World War I from 1914 to 1918, and 8,600 more perished in 1918 when the so-called Spanish flu pandemic spread through the country's population of 1.1 million.

Rankine moved the Flanders and Triumph the short distance to his home, where they sit 55 years later in an eclectic collection of vehicles that includes his first car (a 1927 Chrysler coupe he purchased at the age of 17), a Doble steam car, a 1916 Detroit Electric, a Stutz OHC eight-cylinder Black Hawk coupe, a Bentley Speed Six, and a factory-built 1996 Chevy S-10 that had been converted into an electric pickup. When the retired steam engineer and teacher isn't playing with his impressive barn finds, he is in the air at the rudder of a 1942 de Havilland DH 82 Tiger Moth biplane.

The Triumph has remained untouched to this day, still wearing its original paint, tires, front fender–mounted license plate, and saddlebag.

"It would be a shame to restore it now," Rankine said. "The first owner probably only rode it for two years, then put it away until I bought it in the late 1950s. The bike is almost 100 years old now. I don't want to strip away all of that history."

The Triumph turns out to be slightly younger than the widow thought. She told Rankine it was a 1912 model, but Rankine's son Dallas—a vintage

This is not a barn find, although a young Brian Rankine used many found parts to build it. After seeing plans in a magazine, the New Zealander knew he could engineer a better scooter. *Brian Rankine*

motorcycle expert who ran his own shop for 24 years—researched the Triumph and decided it was a 1913 Model C.

Before committing the information to print with this book, the Rankines consulted the United Kingdom's Vintage Motor Cycle Club, which confirmed it was assembled during October 1912, to 1913 specifications.

Triumph upgraded its bicycle-style chassis for 1913 with a Sturmey-Archer three-speed rear-wheel hub, which the Kiwi bike has. Being produced late in the year makes it a transitional model, though, because it also has the circular exhaust silencer under the magneto that ended with model year 1912. That silencer features a series of holes in a circular plate that is rotated by a foot pedal to allow exhaust gas to escape unrestricted; the device was outlawed the month of the Triumph's build. Its 550cc side-valve single was introduced with the 1910 Model Roadster.

Rankine's large collection of barn finds is all the more amazing when one considers that the country of New Zealand constitutes a remote pair of islands located in the southernmost Pacific Ocean with no domestic auto manufacturing. Rankine's Triumph, for example, was built in Coventry, England, 11,630 miles away—nearly half the earth's circumference—from the shed in which it was found.

"New Zealand has imported just about every type of car and motorcycle imaginable from Europe and America," Rankine said. "In the old days, before the roads were paved, American cars were the most popular because they were sturdier than British or European cars. They just held up better. And it cost so much to import a car this far that people repaired them and kept driving them long after they would in any other country."

As it did in the United States, New Zealand's economy boomed in the 1950s. With increased exports of agricultural products, especially wool, the island country's citizens eagerly discarded long-held souvenirs of the dark World War I years and moved toward the future.

For many Kiwis, it was time to break away from the past, discarding old junk and refuse in lieu of a cleaner, more efficient future. Rankine's Triumph Model C may have been relegated to the dump. How many other vehicles are waiting to be discovered, hauled into the present as a relic of the past?

Brian Rankine's love of motorcycles was apparent from early childhood.

"When I was about 12 years old," he says, "my mother would not let me have a motorbike. She said I was too young to have such a machine."

"I asked her, 'What if I *make* one?'

"She probably thought it would never happen, so she agreed. I had an old *Popular Mechanics* magazine that had plans for a scooter made out of wood, powered with a small Briggs & Stratton engine. I had several goes at this, but it soon became obvious to me that the magazine motorbike would not be very practical.

"I started, in earnest, planning a stronger scooter made out of metal. My father, who was on the medical staff of a local hospital, had no mechanical interest, but I was allowed access to the hospital's plumbing workshop. There I was able to make the frame out of water pipe. Cutting, bending, shaping, and drilling was all done by hand, slowly—then wired together and taken to the local auto service station to get welded.

"I purchased a 350cc Royal Enfield engine and four-speed foot change gearbox. Other parts such as levers, brakes, lights, and fittings came from the local motorbike shop where I spent most of my Friday evenings.

"The front forks were modified from some old girder forks to trailing link to give about four inches of total movement.

"The rear suspension was my own design with twin parallel trailing links. I knew the small wheels would not go well over rough ground, and I wanted a suspension that had plenty of movement. Everything was made to be adjustable, even the steering angles.

"I bolted together various units that I could carry for welding purposes. I don't think my dear mother realized this was going to be the fastest motor scooter in New Zealand when she gave me permission to build my own. I had no formal engineering knowledge, just a natural instinct for how things should be.

"By age 14, I had finished it enough to get a motorcycle license and rode it to college for three years during the 1950s."

KEATING'S KEATING AND OTHER TALES OF DISCOVERY
by Brian Keating

There is a story behind each of the two dozen-plus vintage motorcycles in my museum in Plainfield, New Hampshire, but I probably have the greatest emotional attachment to the one that bears my name. I'm one of those lucky enthusiasts who can see his last name on a list of 20th century motorcycle brands, and I had the great fortune to locate and acquire the only known example of my namesake.

I was always making go-carts powered by lawn mower engines and that kind of thing when I was a kid, which is surprising because no one else in my family had any mechanical inclinations. When I was 15, I picked up a Royal Enfield—a British on/off-road machine from the 1950s—for next to nothing. I put more miles on it pushing it home than actually riding it, but the experience of riding it through the woods got me hooked on two-wheelers.

My first real jump into vintage bikes came in the late 1970s when I was visiting the old Indian Motorcycle Museum in Springfield, Massachusetts, and the curator, Charlie Manthos, was showing me around. Charlie had just bought a basket case from a house fire the day before I arrived, and I could smell the smoke residue in the building. It was a 1946 Indian Chief packed in three bureau drawers and a couple of boxes that smelled strongly of charcoal, but I could see the potential and bought the lot for $500. That Chief became my first restoration and introduced me to the world of the Antique Motorcycle Club of America (AMCA).

I wasn't one for school, so after graduating from high school I started driving trucks. This career gave me the opportunity to do two things I loved: drive and look for old motorcycles in out-of-the-way places.

The combination of vocation and avocation has worked perfectly for me, and I have turned up dozens of hidden treasures over the years.

1948 Harley-Davidson Flathead

The best kind of purchase is the one you make after years of pursuit.

I was driving for UPS in the early 1980s, and I made a delivery out in the boondocks of Lyme, New Hampshire. I asked the 70-year-old lady of the house if she knew of any old motorcycles in the area.

She said that her son had a Harley-Davidson in the farmhouse's basement and asked if I wanted to see it. Of course I did! So we went to the basement where I saw a beautiful unrestored 1948 UL—a springer front suspension mated to a hard tail frame and carrying the final-year Flathead 74-cid V-twin. It was Flight Red with a Connecticut license plate dating back to 1960.

The woman gave me her son's contact information, and I called his home in Connecticut a few weeks later. He said the bike was not for sale, but he gave me permission to visit the bike again and take photos.

Maybe 15 years went by, and I noticed that the old farmhouse with the Harley looked vacant. Guessing that the lady I had delivered the package to that day had passed away, I called her son, who told me he had moved the bike to his home and that it was still not for sale. I tried again to buy it about five years later but, again, no deal.

Finally, 20 years after I first saw it, the Harley's owner agreed to sell it to me, so I drove to Connecticut, where it had been sitting outdoors under a tarp since its relocation from New Hampshire. It really wasn't much worse for wear, but it was a rusty, crusty, ratty, tatty machine, which is the way I like them.

The bike's owner was ready to sell, but his 40-year-old son—stop me if you've heard this before—was there and was adamant that the Harley not leave the family. I left empty-handed but didn't give up on the prospect of one day owning it.

In the summer of 2011, I got a call from my town clerk. She and I have become friends because I'm down there so often registering motorcycles

Brian Keating likes his barn finds to be "rusty, crusty, ratty, tatty." It took Brian Keating 25 years to buy this 1948 Harley-Davidson UL Flathead. He first saw it in the basement of a farmhouse, but it is seen here on the day he purchased it. It had been stored under a tarp behind the owner's house for some time.

and doing paperwork. She said an older gentleman from Connecticut called and was asking for me but could not remember my name; he just knew that somebody who collected old motorcycles lived in Plainfield. The clerk knew me well enough to know that I would want that call, so she gave him my phone number.

The '48 Harley owner called and said he had decided to sell the motorcycle and that his son was okay with it leaving the family. They both felt it was time to let it go to someone who knew how to work on it and enjoy it.

In a way, the iron-head Flathead engine is less desirable than the aluminum-head Panhead engine because the Flathead was on the way out, and it was old technology. To me, though, the rarity of low production and a final-year engine make it very special. From beginning to end, it took 25 years—a quarter of a century—to bring the UL to my garage, but it was worth the wait. It is now a runner and a rider, and I'm keeping it unrestored.

1948 Harley-Davidson Panhead

Another '48 Harley came my way through unusual circumstances, although it only took 10 years for me to buy that one.

A friend of mine knew of an old-timer in New Jersey who owned an unrestored, original-paint Panhead with nice period saddlebags. The old-timer's brother had passed away, and a lot of collectors tried to secure the blue bike from his estate, but he refused to sell. My friend was trying to make a deal and push it my way because he knew I would gladly give him a finder's fee for the trouble. He tried for years but finally gave up and sent me the contact information so I could pursue the bike myself.

I called the surviving brother and explained how I found out about his motorcycle. I asked if it was for sale, and he said, "Kind of."

I told him I had heard it was in good condition and I named a price. He liked the sound of my offer and said it was mine, but he wouldn't tell me where he lived. He just gave me a location and told me to meet him there.

When my son and I pulled into town in my van, I called the owner's number and he drove to our arranged meeting spot. He sized me up, and we chatted about where I was from in New Hampshire. When we met with his approval, he told me to follow him to the house, where he opened the garage door and we saw, buried under miscellaneous junk, the tail of the Harley.

We freed the bike, rolled it into the driveway, and gave it a quick inspection. I told him it was exactly as described and paid him. The deal that had taken a decade to put together took less than 15 minutes to complete, and we were soon headed home with the '48.

It took Brian Keating 10 years to persuade this '48 Harley-Davidson's owner to part with it. Here it is on the day Keating picked it up in New Jersey. The owner did not want to see it running around on the streets near his home, so he purposely sold it to someone far away. Keating happened to be that lucky far-away someone.

Within a few days, word got out that I had scored the Harley that so many others had tried to buy. I finally figured out the old man's reason for letting me buy it—the other collectors were all from New Jersey, and he wanted it to go where he would not see it again. I lucked out by being far enough way to meet his need.

1965 Harley-Davidson FLH Electra Glide

This next one is technically a "Harley in a bus" story.

My friend John Davis was a colorful character who lived in Vermont and had a '65 Harley FLH Electra Glide stored in a school bus on his property.

It was a two-tone blue-and-white, unmolested, unrestored Panhead with a first-year electric start. John was skittish and did not warm up to many people, so it took a while for me to earn his trust. He liked that I appreciated his motorcycle for something more than its monetary value.

John bought the bike new from Wilkins Harley-Davidson in South Barre, Vermont, and rode it some 9,900 miles before parking it in the bus. He didn't want to see it go over the 10,000-mile mark. When I first saw it the bike was weathering well, but its hardware was beginning to rust.

It took me five years to persuade John to sell it to me and give it a permanent home in my collection. By that time, he had moved it into the back of a lockable truck body because more people were becoming aware of the bike and its value. As we pulled it into the daylight, I told him, "John, you will always have visitation rights; you are more than welcome to come over and take it for a ride." When I drove off with it in my van, he had tears in his eyes.

A few years later, he came down and visited the bike, choking up when he saw it. I offered to let him ride it, but he just enjoyed seeing it in its original glory and sitting on it in the driveway. John has since passed away, and I've ridden the bike past its 10,000-mile mark, but I always think about my old friend when I'm enjoying his Electra Glide.

Brian Keating seems to like Harleys that are the first of something or the last of something else. This 1965 Electra Glide marks the final year of the Panhead V-twin; it would be replaced the next year with the company's Shovelhead design.

When Keating first saw the '65 Electra Glide, it was being stored in the back of the school bus. For security, his friend moved it to a lockable truck, where it stayed until Keating bought it.

Romie Lambert

People think I have a lot of crazy machines in my collection, but that's because they didn't have the pleasure of knowing Romie Lambert, now deceased. Romie was ahead of his time as a collector, with a three-story barn in Southampton, Massachusetts, that was full of cars, motorcycles, and even an old Stearman airplane. At one point, I remember seeing three 1956 Porsches covered in branches and leaves, buried up to the axles in dirt.

He was in his sixties when I met him in the late 1980s, and I managed to buy and/or enjoy some historically significant motorcycles through our friendship.

Romie knew Ted Hodgdon, who had worked for the Indian Motorcycle Co., served as president of BSA's North American branch, and was a founding member of the AMCA. When Indian was closing its Springfield factory doors in the early 1950s, Ted called Romie to tell him about the '07 Indian single and a 1943-ish M1 military prototype that he knew Romie would want. The prototype was designed to be dropped out of an airplane by parachute so that a paratrooper could land near it and have ground transportation, but the idea never made it into production.

Another bike of some importance in Romie's barn was a 1954 Norton Manx factory racer he bought from a serviceman who had brought it to the States with the intent to race it before the bike was outlawed by the American Motorcyclist Association in the 1960s.

Romie's Manx had last been raced in Germany on the Hockenheimring Grand Prix track, so it had a competition history. It wore a rare dustbin faring with number plates and came with a toolbox full of spares. Packing a first-year, short-stroke 500cc double-overhead camshaft single, this Manx was unbelievably complete and a very exotic machine for its time. Only a handful of these race-ready 1954 Manxes exist.

The first bike Romie let me buy from him was the military prototype, whose history I thoroughly researched. Even though Indian never made any copies for sale, it was one of several one-off development models documented in the company's prototype registry.

I was happy as a peacock the day he finally let go of the Norton, and Romie seemed pleased when I got it running and paraded it a few times at the Loudon track—what's now called New Hampshire Motor Speedway.

It pays to have friends with friends in high places. Brian Keating purchased this one-off Indian prototype from Romie Lambert, who got it from Indian's Ted Hodgdon after the company closed its doors. The "M1" was developed to be a simple, lightweight mode of transportation for the military. It was intended to be dropped from aircraft for a soldier to use. As such, it is an unbelievably rare piece of Indian history.

Brian Keating's '54 Norton Manx is already rare enough in race form, but the inclusion of a genuine toolbox full of spares makes it a complete historic package. He acquired it from friend Romie Lambert's collection, and the bike has a competition history, having raced at Germany's Hockenheimring Grand Prix track.

Sure, it has four wheels—not two—but it is worth noting that this 1956 Porsche was one of three 356 models sitting in the weeds at Romie Lambert's fabulous and eclectic collection. After Lambert's death the cars, motorcycles, and an airplane were scattered at auction.

I was never able to buy the 1907 Indian, but I worked on it and completed it for Romie. Ted Hodgdon had done most of the work but was never able to complete it. The Indian was one of Romie's prized possessions.

When Romie and his wife died, one of his kids auctioned off everything in that barn, including the '07 Indian.

Keating Wheel Company

I'm retired physically and mentally but not financially. Fortunately for me, I've been able to turn my passion for antiques into a small business and make a living off of vintage motorcycles for the past 15 years. Keating Wheel Co. is not something I made up; it is, in fact, my attempt to keep alive the memory of a small turn-of-the-century bicycle and motorcycle manufacturer whose founder shared my last name.

The Keating Company came out of Holyoke, Massachusetts, and relocated to Middletown, Connecticut, where it made bicycles from 1891 through 1898 or 1899 and built motorcycles from 1901 to 1902.

I own 15 Keating bicycles—most likely the world's largest collection of such—but it took an astounding bit of luck and some real negotiating to put the only known 1902 Keating motorcycle in my collection.

A friend of mine was working on a gentleman's furnace in Woodsville, New Hampshire, in the early 1980s and noticed a lot of mechanical parts scattered about. The homeowner told him it was a Keating motorcycle, which spurred my friend to call me immediately.

I spoke with the owner, who had received the bike from his uncle. He said he intended to restore it, but I talked him out of it and offered to buy it. I couldn't persuade him to part with the Keating for mere cash, but he did offer to trade it for another motorcycle—one that I didn't happen to have.

It took more than a year to make the deal happen, but I located the motorcycle he wanted, bought it (from a very reluctant owner), and traded it for the Keating. I was on pins and needles the whole year that arrangement was coming together.

There was very little information available on the Keating brand. I had been advertising in the AMCA club newsletter since the 1970s that I was looking for anything related to the Keating motorcycle, and people told me there was no such thing. "We'd all like to own a motorcycle named after ourselves," they told me, "but it just doesn't exist."

Now that it's sitting here on display in my living room, I can tell you it very well does exist. Keating's foray into the motorcycle market is powered by a four-stroke single displacing about 200cc with inlet over

Few collectors can claim a bike with their name on it, but Brian Keating managed to find and secure the only known 1902 Keating motorcycle. It was in pieces scattered around a basement when a friend told him about it. After a year of negotiating, he finally convinced the owner to sell.

exhaust. It has a two-piece frame and is chain driven. The gas tank sits right on top of the engine inlet, which is fed not by a carburetor but a vaporizer. In an unusual but attractive styling choice, the exhaust runs through the rear fender.

I've never had it running, but I plan to make that happen someday. There is very little paint left on the metal—some remnants of black on the engine cases, blue on the fuel tank. It would be nice if some sales literature were to make its way into my collection that listed the color choices.

Although the first Keating Wheel Co. went out of business immediately after the introduction of its motorcycle line, it is worth noting that its development and production happened before Mr. Harley and Mr. Davidson turned out their first experiment. (Heck, it even took place before Orville and Wilbur got their Wright Flyer off the ground at Kitty Hawk.)

There is even a substantial, documented connection between Keating, Indian, and Harley motorcycles: Keating sued both companies for misuse of patents—Indian in 1906 and H-D in 1917—and won both cases.

TRIUMPH OVER NATURE

When Triumph restorer Gregg Rammel found his 1966 TT Special racer sitting behind a barn in Michigan, natural forces were actively attempting to reclaim the British motorcycle. As in any compelling story about archaeological discoveries, this one involved a lot of digging.

Rammel first learned of TT Specials in 1971 when the 15-year-old enthusiast went to work for a Triumph shop in Detroit. The other, older guys told him about the TT's legendary power and handling abilities.

They said it was a bike that was hard to beat when it was new, and each one of them had owned one.

Triumph's American west coast distributor, Pasadena, California–based Johnson Motors (aka "JoMo"), had the marketing muscle to persuade BSA Automotive Division Chief Executive Edward Turner in Meriden, West Midlands, England, to build U.S.-specific models.

The Johnson Motors dealership had been aggressively selling and racing Triumph motorcycles since 1937 and had enormous influence over the brand's home office. JoMo's myriad wins on flat tracks, beaches, salt flats, and desert

Here is Greg Rammel's 1966 Triumph TT Special shortly after he pulled it from behind an old farm building. It was in amazingly good condition to have been sitting outdoors unprotected for a decade. The stained tires show where the ground was trying to reclaim the bike.

107

Surface rust was the biggest problem Rammel had to overcome during his TT Special's restoration. The aluminum engine parts had oxidized and "looked like they were growing fur."

courses encouraged Triumph's Turner to create powerful motorcycles with American names like Bonneville, Thunderbird, and Daytona.

Bobby Turner (no relation to Triumph's Turner) rode a JoMo-modified 650cc Thunderbird to 132.26 miles per hour at Bonneville in 1951—an AMA Class C speed that would not be surpassed until seven years later. A JoMo Triumph T120 managed 135.74 mph at Bonneville.

Jimmy Phillips, Ed Kretz Sr., and Ed Kretz Jr. rode Triumphs to victories in every type of competition, giving the bike maker the kind of exposure and reputation that no ad copy could possibly generate.

JoMo's success gave birth in 1963 to the TT Special, a performance package available on the Triumph Bonneville T120C, the company's bare-bones competition model. Ordering the T120C TT Special gave the buyer the Bonneville's powerful 650cc vertical twin engine, but on a chassis stripped of all street-legal components and fitted with a straight exhaust that exited directly ahead of the rear tire. Added for 1965, a revised system in which the twin pipes met under the engine and ran the centerline of the bike to blast out hot exhaust aimed at the rear tire came to be known as the "TT pipes." (In true racing fashion, TT pipes prevented the use of a center stand.)

What a difference a few boxes of NOS (new old stock) parts makes! The one-year-only aluminum fenders were the hardest pieces to locate. Triumph's 1966 TT Special was a British-made bike created largely for the American market. The company took care of its own east coast distribution, but the west coast was covered by Johnson Motors of Pasadena, California. "JoMo" aggressively promoted sales and competition of Triumph motorcycles since importing the first bikes in 1937.

Rammel's TT engine serial number reads T120 TT DU 39576. Triumph engine numbers had prefixes indicating the model type, followed by the sequential serial number. "DU" indicates this was a unit-construction model. Triumph serial numbers for the 1966 model year ran from DU 24875 through DU 44393.

Unlike the café racers, Triumph's TTs were fitted with wide handlebars that gave the rider leverage for maneuvering around flat tracks. All 1966 TTs came from the factory with this white-and-orange paint scheme.

The TT had a unique exhaust system that ran both pipes under the crankcase down the centerline of the engine, and the twin pipes exited straight into the rear tire.

For 1966, Triumph introduced the TT Special as its own model—a factory hot rod with a lightweight frame, the Bonneville's pushrod, overhead-valve 650; a pair of high-flow carburetors; open exhaust pipes; and 11:1 compression. Aimed squarely at the U.S. market, it was imported stripped-down and race-ready with low gearing: longer, undrilled aluminum fenders and no lights. There was no speedometer—just a tach.

The TT diet extended to the electrical system, which had no battery. Triumph's "energy transfer ignition" featured a five-wire stator that generated its own spark through the kick starter. All '66 TT Specials were white with an orange stripe down the length of the gas tank.

Light and powerful, the TT Special became a favorite among competitors at Ascot Park speedway in Gardena, California. Drag racers liked it as well. Hard-charging racers like Steve McQueen, Bud Ekins, Gene Romero, and Gary Nixon all rode TTs, which were more than adequate against the Harleys and BSAs of the time.

As JoMo had promised Triumph, the TT Special was a strong seller, even among non-racers who installed Triumph headlight kits to make them legal for the street.

Gregg Rammel had memorized all these details and dreamed of owning a TT since the early days of his work at the Triumph dealership. When the

Today, Rammel devotes his garage time to Ducatis, such as this 1974 750 SS, which he considers to be "the Holy Grail of Ducatis."

shop closed in 1980, Rammel took his tools home and started working on Triumphs, Ducatis, and other makes, from his garage.

Fast forward to October 1986. Rammel was specializing in the restoration of 1966–1970 Triumphs and had seven bikes in his collection. But there was something missing from his garage.

"I had been looking for a TT Special for years," he said. "When the guys at the shop first told me about them back in the 1970s, I thought, 'Man, I want to get my hands on one of those,' but they were hard to find.

"Then, in 1986, one just fell into my lap."

A customer told Rammel about an old motorcycle sitting behind a barn in Romeo, Michigan, that might be a Triumph and was possibly a TT Special. Rammel wasted no time tracking down the owner and asking a ton of questions.

The seller said the bike was, indeed, a TT Special and that it had been parked on his property for 10 years. If Rammel was interested, it was his for $20.

"The owner didn't have anything to share with me about its history, or even how it got there—just that he would be glad to see it go.

"The part about only wanting $20 made me think it was probably in such sorry shape that I would be wasting my time to drive the hour and a half to look at it," said Rammel, "but I couldn't take a chance on losing a restorable TT."

Once in Romeo, Rammel found a severely neglected bike whose VIN checked out as a genuine 1966 TT Special.

"I could see why he thought $20 was a fair asking price," Rammel said. "This thing was buried up to the frame in mud and had been sitting outside, unprotected, for a decade.

"It was nasty. The exhaust pipe was solid rust, as were the chain guard, chain, rims, and shocks. The aluminum parts looked like fur was growing on them. Even though it was fall, weeds were still clinging to it.

"A previous owner must have used it on the street because someone had installed a light kit. The stock handlebar—a wide piece to give leverage for steering on dirt tracks—had been replaced with a semi-high design, which was popular for street riding in the 1970s. It was wearing the remains of a custom paint job, and the front fender was missing."

Rammel found a shovel on the property and started excavating to free his prize. He loaded the muddy TT into his van, slid $20 under the front door of the farmer (who had long since disappeared), and headed back to his garage. (He later received a piece of paper in the mail from the seller that read: Received from Gregg Rammel $20 for 1966 Triumph motorcycle.)

Awaiting his rusty find were boxes of new/old stock Triumph TT parts Rammel had been buying and saving for just such an occasion. He photographed the TT in its "barn fresh" state and began dismantling it.

"As I suspected," he said, "the motor was seized up, and the pistons had become one piece with the cylinders.

"I found a new cylinder and TT pistons. All the aluminum had to be bead blasted and wire brushed to bring back the original texture. The outer covers had to be polished, and I re-chromed a few odds and ends.

"The fenders were tricky, because the 1966 TT used aluminum, which cracked easily, but Triumph switched to stainless steel the next year. Finding the right aluminum fenders without extra holes drilled in them to run wires for street-legal taillights was very difficult.

"I took time to ensure that every nut and bolt was correct. When I finished the bike, the only thing that wasn't from 1966 England was the air in the tires."

Rammel's '66 was restored to be the perfect track bike. When finished, he fired it up, tore up and down the street a few times, performed a few 1960s-style holeshot launches, then put it away.

"I haven't started it in 15 years, but it would be ready to go if I put gas in it. I've gotten it out recently for some shows, including the Motorcycle Meet in Madison, Wisconsin, last year. It seems a lot of people are like me, and they really wanted one of these when they were kids and couldn't afford one—or didn't have any business being on one."

Today, the TT is displayed alongside a 1972 Triumph Hurricane, a 1967 Triumph TR6C, and a 1951 Vincent Black Shadow in a temperature- and humidity-controlled room, protected from the outdoor environment that once tried to destroy it.

THE VINTAGE CYCLE MASTER

No book about motorcycle barn-finds would be complete without a number of pages dedicated to Dale Walksler, proprietor of the Wheels Through Time Museum in Maggie Valley, North Carolina.

Walksler, a retired Illinois Harley-Davidson dealer, was collecting cool old bikes—mostly Harleys and Indians—long before it was popular. Walksler was 15 years old when he bought his first vintage Harley-Davidson, a 1952 Panhead, for $250 in 1970.

Since then he has been selectively acquiring barn-find bikes, and in most cases deciding to leave them in unrestored condition. His collection now numbers more than 300 unique American motorcycles, which he displays in his museum in scenes that rival Disney World.

The man never stops. These days he is still dragging home barn-finds, but not just any barn-find; Walksler is refining his collection, picking carefully, selling off lesser machines, and adding bikes that better lend themselves to his museum themes. Here are summaries of his latest acquisitions:

1919 Fastmotor

Lots of rare barn-find bikes are discovered in, well, barns, but others are discovered in garages, warehouses, basements, and abandoned buildings—everyone reading this book knows this already. But Dale Walksler stole one of his most significant barn-finds right from under the noses of 3,000 experts at the Mid-American Auction in Las Vegas in 2011.

Here's how he pulled off the caper.

Walksler goes to the auction every year, along with every other serious motorcycle collector on this hemisphere. Walksler brought two Harleys to sell at this auction, a 1913 and a 1932. It was Wednesday, and the auction didn't begin until Thursday, so after Walksler unloaded the bikes from his truck, he and friend Mike Lang decided to walk around and check out the other bikes that were going to the auction block over the next three days.

Walksler's buddy Lang—a Harley racing expert—noticed a bike several aisles over and said, "Hey Dale, that 1919 over there sure looks good."

So Walksler said, "Let's go take a look at it."

As the two got closer, the old bike looked sad, sitting on flat tires. Dale bent down and really gave it a good inspection: it had original paint, but the carburetor had an airsleeve, which was not a standard item for this motorcycle.

It was a 1919 Electric model, which meant it was a civilian street bike with an electric headlight, taillight, and horn. But the curious thing about this bike was the airsleeve. It stuck in his mind as an important clue. It was mounted on the left-hand side of the bike, and immediately below that was the engine serial number. "Suddenly I realized that I had found something very, very special," Walksler said. "This bike was equipped with a factory-built racing engine. But the interesting thing was this was not a racing bike."

Walksler concluded the engine was built in Harley-Davidson's racing department but the bike was not, and that a racing engine on a street bike made this a one-of-a-kind machine. It was probably a special order for an enthusiast sometime before the Great Depression.

According to Walksler, serial numbers on racing engines had three digits that ran between 500 and 999. When he noticed the serial number on this engine was 595, he knew he had a winner. "My stomach turned upside down realizing that in the next few days at least 3,000 people were going to walk past this bike and also realize what an incredible motorcycle it was," he said.

Remember we mentioned that Walksler liked themes in his museum? Well, one of those themes is for original-paint Harleys from the teens. He owned a 1913, 1914, 1915, 1917, and 1918. He was missing a 1916 and a 1919. Recently he found and purchased a 1916 ("The rarest dang '16 I've ever seen"), which left him missing only the '19.

"So I'm thinking to myself, 'God, if I could get this bike, it would complete my collection of original-paint, teens Harleys,'" he said. "It would be the ideal piece for my collection, but how will I ever buy it with all these experts here?"

Worst of all, of the 500 bikes to be auctioned off at this show, this particular bike wouldn't come to the block until 7 p.m. Saturday, the sixth bike from the end of the auction. The organizers also knew how rare the bike was.

Walksler didn't sleep well on Wednesday night. Or Thursday night. On Friday, his two bikes sold, which meant he had the cash to pursue the 1919, at least until the bidding got really high.

On Friday of auction weekend, Walksler came upon friend, Bill Rodencal, who works for the Harley-Davidson archives office. Walksler describes him as a very, very sharp guy. "His sole purpose for being at the auction was to buy one particular bike for the Harley museum, and he had no interest in the 1919," Walksler said. "So I said to Bill, 'Boy, that sure is a nice 1919 over there,' and Bill said back to me with a wink, 'Yes, and if there is anything you'd like to know about it, let me know.'

"And we both smiled, knowing the bike was very special, but we never discussed it again that weekend."

Both Walksler and Rodencal understood the bike's value, but how many others had any idea?

Saturday arrived and several big players in the motorcycle collecting world were hovering around the bike. Walksler is well known in that world, so often

Miller Barko, a West Virginia coal miner, bought this rarer than rare Harley Fastmotor new in 1919. Current owner Dale Walksler said it is a true gentleman's speed machine, a big racing engine mounted on a civilian street bike. *Brad Bowling*

his interest in a particular bike drives the prices higher as other bidders take notice. For that reason, Walksler had his son, Matt, bid on the '19 instead.

The bidding was still fast and furious, and Matt was not yet the expert that his dad was, so at some point, Walksler tapped his son on the shoulder and took over the bidding. He has a favorite spot he likes to sit in during the auction, but this time—in an effort to be more anonymous—he sat in a different location. It still didn't help.

"Toward the end, it was hard to tell where the bids were coming from," he said. "But I ended up being the successful bidder at $43,000. As I rolled my new bike off the podium, and toward my little spot near the Wheels Through Time Museum display, Jeff Ray and Brian Slark from the Barber Museum came over and asked, 'Did you buy that bike?' I told them I had. Jeff said, 'That was a good one,' and I said, 'Jeff, if you only knew.'"

In the end, only Rodencal and Walksler knew just how special this bike was.

After he purchased the bike and pushed it over to his display, a man approached him and thanked him for purchasing it. He had been the owner who consigned the bike to the auction. He purchased it in 1995.

Walksler's collection of original-paint Harleys from the "teens" was missing only a 1919. Having purchased this highly unusual model at a Las Vegas auction now makes his collection complete. *Brad Bowling*

"Now here's the story," said Walksler. "This guy sold windows in Pennsylvania. An elderly woman called him to price out a couple of new windows she wanted installed in her house. While he was installing the windows, he walked into the garage with the woman. There was a 1960s Pontiac parked in there.

"You should buy old Millie," she said. "It's my old car and I don't drive it anymore."

So he bought the car. While they were at the title transfer office, she said, "Oh, and you should buy old Nellie, too."

The man asked, "Who's Nellie?"

She explained that Nellie was her deceased husband's old motorcycle. So they walked back to the garage, and next to where the Pontiac was parked, but under cover and out of sight, was the 1919 Harley-Davidson.

She explained that her husband, Miller Barko, purchased the bike new in 1919 and stopped riding it in 1929. He parked it in the garage, where it sat from 1929 until 1995.

Walksler did some investigation about Miller Barko. He was a coal miner in the late teens. He made a good salary and bought the most expensive motorcycle of the time—a special, hand-built model that shared virtually no parts with a standard road engine. Harley started racing in 1914, and the basis of all their racing engines into the 1920s was the 1914-style, narrow case, roller-bearing design.

According to Walksler, this bike was certainly special ordered. Reconnecting with Bill Rodencal of Harley-Davidson, they determined that the bike could not have been offered on a standard order form. There is not another Fastmotor Electric model that has ever been built.

What makes this bike a hybrid is the fact that it has a generator. All other racing models have a magneto, which requires an acetolene headlight. But because of the electric lights and horn, this model required a generator in order to recharge the battery.

"This was truly a gentleman's speed machine," Walksler said.

As he was driving home to Maggie Valley, North Carolina, from Las Vegas, Walksler opened the side door of his van to inspect his new treasure while he was refueling. The sunshine was strong and allowed Walksler to see Miller Barko's initials printed on the front fender in an Old English type style.

"I immediately called the previous owner, the window salesman, to ask if he had ever noticed the initials," he said. "He said that even though he had owned the bike for 15 years, he had never noticed them.

"So the bike went into the Barko garage in 1919 and was removed in 1995. Then it went into the window salesman's garage from 1995 to 2011. Now it's in my museum in Maggie Valley."

And Dale confirms that finding and purchasing a rare bike among a building full of experts is truly the barn-find of them all.

This 1913 Harley-Davidson Is a Pisser

"Sometime in December 2010, I received a phone call from a woman who said she had inherited a 1913 Harley-Davidson," Walksler said. "After a few minutes of speaking with her, I realized this was probably a true story. An insane, multi-layered, true story."

The woman's family name was Hawthorne, and she lived in Elgin, Illinois, also home of the Elgin Watch Company. She told Walksler about her grandfather, who was an executive at the watch company. And according to family folklore, he purchased a new Harley-Davidson motorcycle in 1913—almost 100 years ago. She explained to Walksler, who happens to be a history buff, that her surname Hawthorne goes all the way back to Nathanial Hawthorne, renowned early American author and short-story writer.

Around 1913, the Elgin area was a hotbed of Harley-Davidson activity because of its proximity, about 60 miles, to Milwaukee, where the bikes were manufactured. Most riders in the Chicago area purchased their bikes from CH Lang, who, according to Walksler, sold roughly 40 percent of Harley's total production out of his dealership. Chicago was quite a hub of motorcycle activity at the time, and the most exotic bike one could be seen riding was the new Harley, in its third year of producing twin-cylinder bikes, which now also featured chain drive instead of belt drive. They were reliable and powerful machines.

The woman's grandfather eventually passed ownership of the 1913 Harley onto one of his sons, her uncle. At one point, her uncle had been an executive with Elgin Watch Company as well, but over the last 25 years of his life, he became a recluse, seldom leaving his mansion, even though the water, electricity, and heat had been turned off and the building condemned years earlier.

Her uncle died in 2010, so she was called to go through the house and settle his estate. She had heard about a motorcycle he once owned, but had never seen it and imagined that it had been disposed of years earlier.

When she entered the garage, she saw some old motorcycle parts against the back wall, but to get to them, she had to make a path through nearly 2,000 old whiskey bottles. They weren't empty, but they didn't have liquor in them. She discovered her reclusive uncle used to drink the whiskey, then urinate in the bottles. Instead of throwing them out, he stored them. Inside the house were another 2,000 urine-filled whiskey bottles.

After hearing the bizarre story, Walksler had to see and acquire the motorcycle parts as quickly as possible, even if it meant running a gauntlet of 50-year-old urine bombs. He called his father, who lives in the Chicago area, and even though he is not a bike guy, could at least survey the contents and report back to his son.

Walksler asked his father, Bernie, to drive over to the woman's house and see everything for himself. His father agreed, and the next day, December 10, 2010, he drove to Elgin and met the woman. It ended up as an all-day affair, as he had to endure the Hawthorne family story, the Elgin Watch Company story, the whiskey bottle story, and so on. It turns out she was nearly as reclusive as her uncle and desperately needed the money that selling her uncle's assets could produce.

Walksler's father made good notes and at the end of the day reported back to his son with descriptions and photos of the pieces. The photos proved that it was a 1913 Harley, but it was completely disassembled. The engine was still mounted on the frame, but the fenders, front fork, handlebars, and all the little parts were dirty and crusty and smelly, no doubt through contact with the contents of the whiskey bottles.

"When I got the photos from my dad, I called the lady and we struck a deal," Walksler said. "We agreed on $18,000 for her pile of crap, so the next Saturday I climbed into my trusty minivan and drove the 12 hours to Chicago."

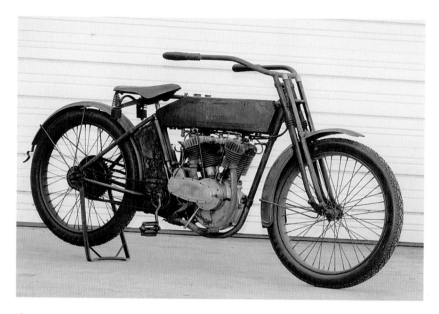

The 1913 Harley that almost slipped through Walksler's fingers. The bike sat for generations in a decrepit Illinois garage surrounded by trash and liquor bottles. When discovered, it was disassembled, dirty, crusty, and smelly. *Brad Bowling*

He spent that evening visiting with his dad and making a few phone calls. He should have noticed that he missed a lot of calls that night, but he wanted to spend quality time with his father.

"We got up early Sunday morning and decided that we wouldn't take a chance; we were going to call Ms. Hawthorne and tell her we'd like to pick up the bike a day earlier than we had planned," Walksler said. But before he called the woman, he figured he'd first check his voice mail. One call was from Barry Kohagen of Barry's Cycles in Decatur, Illinois. Walksler has been friends with Kohagen for 20 years.

"Hello, Dale, this is Barry," the voice mail said. "I hope you are not mad at me. I'm up near Elgin talking to Mrs. Hawthorne about the '13 Harley. I'm going to buy the bike. Call me. Bye."

Walksler was dumbfounded.

"I didn't call Hawthorne because obviously the bike was already in Barry's hands," Walksler said. "My first call was to Barry."

Walksler surmised that Hawthorne desperately needed money. She was about 55 years old and had a son in his twenties. Her son must have reasoned with her, "Look, Mom, we need the money. We can't care about some guy from Maggie Valley." He then picked up the phone and called Barry's Cycles.

It was never Walksler's desire to restore the bike, just to make it a running, operating bike again. The original paint and lettering was still in decent condition. *Brad Bowling*

"After hearing the story, I had an idea," Walksler said. He called Kohagen with one word in mind: "partners."

"What do you mean we're partners?" Kohagen said.

Kohagen called his friend Denny, then called Walksler back to say that they agreed that they would be partners on the Harley.

"I made the suggestion that I would take the motorcycle back to Maggie Valley, totally rebuild it, then take it to Las Vegas in January for the auction," Walksler said. "The three of us would split the profits as partners.

"Barry is an interesting guy who has a huge respect for vintage motorcycles," said Walksker. "But he would have been out of his league putting this thing back together. He quickly realized the value I could bring to the table. It was a good business decision on his part."

What Walksler didn't know when he called Kohagen that Sunday morning was just how tired his friend had become. "Barry lives in Decatur, which is about three hours from Chicago," he said. "By the time he met with this woman, who lived in Geneva, then drove to Elgin to see the bike, then to Geneva again to complete his negotiations, then to Elgin, then back home to Decatur, he didn't get home until four in the morning. So with four hours sleep I'm telling him that we're partners. No wonder he agreed so fast."

Walksler drove to Kohagen's house and did a summary of all the parts. Even though the bike had been virtually disassembled for at least 50 years, just about everything was there to turn it into a motorcycle again.

"Barry already owns a 1912 Harley, so based on his familiarity of his own bike, he was able to identify nearly every nut, bolt, and washer over a 12-hour period."

It was not Walksler's intention to restore the bike—the original paint was in decent condition—but only to make it a running, operating motorcycle again. "I got home about 10 p.m.," he said. "By 4 a.m., I had the engine out and the bottom end rebuilt. It was then that I knew I could have this bike completed in a week.

"When I got it done, it ran like new," Walksler said. "It ran so good you could have ridden it on the Cannonball cross country rally."

Walksler added a few missing pieces from his collection of bits, but every nut, bolt, and component is original Harley-Davidson. "You could never tell that bike had been apart," he said. But even though the threads were cleaned, those nuts and bolts were left greasy.

An original 1913 Harley—what's it worth? The only way to know for sure would be to put it on eBay or bring it to a public auction. Since there are so many knowledgeable buyers at the Mid America auction in Las Vegas, the partners agreed that it would be the best place to dispose of their investment. But they had decided so late, it was not possible to have the bike featured in any pre-event publicity or even in the auction catalogue.

Regardless, bidding was rapid. The price quickly rose and the hammer came down at $80,000. "After subtracting the costs of restoring the bike and bringing it to Las Vegas, we probably split a $50,000 profit for one week's work," Walksler added.

"Since I already owned a 1913, even if I would have bought this bike, I would have sold the bike anyway," Walksler said. "But the story here is that even though someone bought a bike out from someone else, nobody got hurt.

"There was a happy ending."

1916 Sidecar Harley-Davidson

"This motorcycle is driven from the sidecar," Walksler said. "It's the craziest thing I've ever seen."

About five years ago, Walksler started receiving phone calls from friends asking if he had seen the 1916 Harley-Davidson motorcycle that was going up for auction in Pennsylvania. So he jumped online and realized that it was one of the most special motorcycles he had seen in his life.

The driver actually drove the vehicle from the sidecar.

"When the bike came up for sale, I was in no financial position to afford a rare bike that was obviously on the radar of every major collector in the world," Walksler said. "However, I decided that I would bid on it anyway. I'd just call in my bid. That's when I was told that bidders had to place their bids in person; no phone bids."

It was a typical farm auction—with an eccentric collection of 70 or 80 collector cars and one motorcycle. Walksler began investigating the bike, but could find nothing. From the photographs, though, he realized that it was very special and something he would like to add to his museum. But he had to come to terms with the fact that he was not in a position to be a serious buyer. "I had to write it off," he said. "I stay close to the guys at the Barber Museum in Birmingham, Alabama, Brian Slark and Jeff Ray, and I knew they would probably go up to bid on this bike. So I called the Museum the day before the auction to say hello to Jeff and the receptionist said he wasn't in. I knew where he was—on the way up to Pennsylvania for the auction."

Walksler decided to have some fun. He called Jeff Ray's cell phone and asked where he was. "I'm on the road," Ray told him.

Walksler asked what exit he was at.

"322."

"No kidding," Walksler said. "I'm at exit 300. I'll see you at the auction tomorrow."

"We had a good laugh over that. I told him I was just joking around, that I wasn't really going to the auction."

Walksler heard about the auction second-hand; there was a small group of people interested in the vintage cars, but there were at least 200 people there to buy one motorcycle. The rumors of this bike had caught like wildfire among the motorcycle collecting community. The Barber Museum was there to buy the unusual bike. So was the Harley-Davidson Museum. And the National Motorcycle Museum. Even the *American Pickers* television show was there to document the event. Every serious motorcycle collector on the East Coast was at the auction.

Then a funny thing happened.

A collector at the auction lived in the same Pennsylvania neighborhood the auction was being held. He was a novice collector who specialized mostly in 1930s, 1940s, and 1950s bikes. This collector was clever, but really cautious.

"He walked into the auction and observed all the chaos and realized two things," Walksler said. "He had the financial wherewithal to own this bike, and he was as good as anyone else in the room. He became adamant that this machine was not going to leave this neighborhood. He raised his hand, and raised his hand, and raised his hand."

In the end, he had outbid everybody else in the room when he raised his hand at a final $87,000 bid. A virtual stranger walked away with one of that year's most intriguing motorcycle discoveries. Nobody knew who the guy was, and nobody knew where the bike was going. Walksler supposed that the bike had slipped forever into a private collection, never to be seen again.

Three years later, Walksler was at a large swap meet and was approached by a man. The two had a little chat, and the man introduced himself as Ed.

"I'm the guy who bought the 1916 Harley sidecar bike in Pennsylvania," he told Walksler.

"Man, it's nice to meet you," Walksler said. "Listen, if you'd ever like to get that bike running, I'd like to help. It would be an honor to work on that Harley." No promise was made, and the two parted ways.

Another year later, Walksler saw a familiar man walking through the Wheels Through Time Museum, but couldn't place him. Then he realized it was Ed.

Walksler gave Ed a guided tour through the collection. At the conclusion of the tour, Ed turned to Walksler and said, "Dale, my sidecar bike belongs here."

"I knew that the moment I first saw a picture of it," Walksler said, who then showed Ed exactly where he would display the bike if he were ever lucky enough to own it.

Over time, the two became friends and saw each other at the major swap meets. They began to talk about the possibility of trading bikes so that Ed would have motorcycles he was more familiar with, and the rare sidecar bike would end up at Wheels Through Time.

"Then things got real interesting," Walksler said.

The two had preliminary negotiations on a trade that would include no cash. Walksler would trade several bikes from his collection for the '16 Harley. Then he made the mistake of introducing Ed to a friend, a gentleman from Kansas whose family happened to own one of the largest stashes of old Harley bikes and parts in the world.

"Ed and I were now friends, so I made the introduction," Walksler said. "I'm always helping people, so I told him, 'There is a collection out in Kansas that you might want to visit.'

"So he goes out there and ends up giving them an opportunity to come and look at the sidecar bike for potential trade."

Soon thereafter, Walksler drove up to Pennsylvania for the swap meet. He brought two of the three bikes he and Ed had discussed for the trade toward his sidecar bike. He drove directly to Ed's house. In a terrific twist, the fellow from Kansas arrived at the house at the very same time. "It was an awkward time for all of us," Walksler said. "Rather than make Ed any more uncomfortable, I decided to just leave and go to the swap meet. I told Ed I'd see him at the swap meet, and left.

"I've always looked at deals like this: If it works, it works. If I don't end up with the bike, then it wasn't meant to be." Walksler felt Ed was a worthy collector in his own right and would make the best choice for the bike.

He was correct. After Walksler left, no deal was struck between Ed and the man from Kansas. Soon thereafter, Walksler renegotiated and delivered three bikes to Ed and took home the prize. "Ed is a businessman, and he made an $85,000 investment four years earlier and wanted to show a profit on the motorcycle," Walksler said. "We evaluated the three bikes I had and danced around with the current value of the sidecar bike. In the end, we both made a pretty happy deal. He's a man with strong moral integrity. He honestly felt that it would be much more important that people enjoy his machine at the Wheels Through Time Museum than have it sitting in his garage."

The Sidecar Bike

The research on this intriguing bike is not yet complete. Harley-Davidson's Bill Redenzel has invited Walksler to his company's archives to try to identify the motorcycle's work orders in the files. According to Walksler, the bike must be driven from the sidecar, but it is not handicap-equipped.

"The driver is required to use both arms and legs to operate this machine," Walksler said. "My suspicion is that it was factory-built prior to World War I for a lady. It has a canopy top, which would have been suitable for a lady, or maybe a midget who couldn't ride a traditional motorcycle."

According to Walksler, the '16 is basically a stock electric model, which is a higher-end model than a magneto-equipped model. It has a factory, Harley-Davidson–built sidecar attachment—actually, it's a double sidecar. "At that time, Harley was in the sidecar business," Walksler said. "The interesting thing about this double sidecar is that it has a footrest up close to the seat, almost like it was built for a child or a very short person. I truly believe that this bike was built for an enthusiast, for someone who wanted to enjoy the joy of riding a motorcycle but couldn't."

On a standard 1916 Harley, the carburetor is mounted on the left side, but on this bike, it is mounted on the right side, facing the sidecar. And even though there is an opening door on the right side of the sidecar, there is a door opening on the left, allowing the rider to make fuel adjustments while driving. No one knows if Harley built more than one sidecar-driven bike.

Since the bike has a 1921 New Jersey license plate, Walksler hopes to find some information on the bike and the owner through searching New

One of the most unusual motorcycles Walksler has come across in all his years of collecting, this 1916 Harley, was built to be driven from the sidecar, not the motorcycle. It has an usual, long handlebar that reaches into the sidecar, foot pedals, and an engine access panel for carburetor adjustments while on the road. *Brad Bowling*

This instrument panel is mounted on the extended handlebar that reaches into the passenger compartment. *Brad Bowling*

Jersey motor vehicle records. Also, he is confident that a photo of the bike must exist in one of the four weekly motorcycle magazines between 1916 and 1921. "I have hundreds of those old magazines, but I don't have all of them," he said.

Walksler was patient in acquiring the bike, and is confident that patience—and a lot of hard work—will yield more answers for the Harley Sidecar Bike.

1929 Board Track/Dirt Track Racer

Walksler's 1929 barn-find racer didn't win in the Preservation Class at Pebble Beach. That honor went to "The World's Fastest Indian," but Walksler's bike took third in class.

Walksler's interest in the bike began in 1990, during a road trip from Santa Fe to Denver for a swap meet. He was traveling with his friend Daniel Statnekov, one of the world's foremost experts in American board track racing, an early American style of racing on banked, wooden tracks.

Along the way, Statnekov realized they'd be passing one of his favorite sites. "You know, I haven't told a lot of people about this stash of motorcycles I discovered in Kansas," he said. "You wouldn't believe it: buildings, basements, attics, and silos filled with motorcycle parts. It's one of the most amazing places I've been in my life. And there is this one orange bike there . . ."

Statnekov told Walksler of a board track racer that had no engine.

"The owner wouldn't sell it to me, even though I offered him a fair price for it," he said.

Over the years, Walksler and Statnekov occasionally discussed the bike. It intrigued Walksler because apparently the engine didn't mount vertically, like a J-model, but horizontally, like a Panhead or a Knucklehead. And Walksler, forever chasing original-paint Harleys, was excited to hear that the orange paint looked original.

About nine years after first hearing about the bike, Walksler was in Kansas picking through another large stash of parts when he overheard a conversation that included: "I heard that the old man died in such-and-such a town."

"This triggered my brain's hard drive and the conversation that Daniel and I had years earlier about the orange board track racer," he said.

Soon enough, Walksler was driving back from the Las Vegas auction with his girlfriend when he said, "We're going to take a detour into central Kansas. There is an old motorcycle there I want to find."

"Detour" isn't quite accurate. It was an entirely separate trip. It included turning off Highway 50 and driving hundreds of miles in a huge windstorm pulling a trailer. Driving into Dodge City, home of the Dodge City Classic motorcycle races of the 1920s, he came to a realization. "God, this bike and Dodge City are so close, maybe there is a connection," he said.

Driving within 30 miles of town, Walksler took out his cell phone and called directory assistance. He was given the man's phone number by the operator. He called.

Walksler's heart was pounding. Soon he would be talking to the person who owned not only the orange board track racer, but also a huge stash of parts.

The man's son answered. "I told him I had just driven 14 hours off the Interstate, and is there any way I could take a look at his dad's stuff," he said. "I told him that I had once met his dad at the Davenport swap meet and thought he was a really good guy. I told him I was not a 'bone-picker,' but would be honored to see his collection."

"We're not letting anyone in," said the man's son. "We've had a lot of people calling to pick on Dad's bones." Walksler said he understood that, but that he was a historian and owned a museum in Maggie Valley.

"Oh . . . my brother has heard of your place," said the son.

"We got along well on the phone and he had a nice voice, so I was optimistic," Walksler said. They agreed to meet the next morning at 9 a.m. to see his father's stash. Walksler got right to the point.

"I'm a straight shooter," he said. "I'm honored to see your father's stuff, but I'm interested in seeing the old racing bike."

"We still have it," the son said.

Driving onto the family's farm, there was no sign of motorcycles anywhere, just farm buildings and junk cars everywhere. Walksler was brought directly into the father's house. Walking through the back door, he entered a pantry. Hanging from the ceiling, directly above the freezer, was the orange board track racer.

"It was a genuine Harley-Davidson board track racer, but an unknown version because of its unique frame, hanging there with no engine," Walksler said. "I inspected it carefully and showed the son the unusual motor mount. I don't know if it's been modified, but it sure was interesting."

They spent the next eight hours looking around the property. The father was indeed a packrat, having stuffed bikes and parts in every nook and cranny.

"It's *cold*, and my girlfriend wouldn't leave the van," Walksler said. "As the sun was going down, I made him an offer. I actually had a beautiful 1962 Corvette in my trailer, so I offered that in trade.

"I said, 'I'll trade you this car for a bunch of this stuff,' but the son said,

'We just don't have anywhere to store it because all the barns and buildings are full.' But we were getting along well."

As it was getting darker and colder, the conversation turned to the orange bike. "Of everything I've seen today—all the Harleys and Indians—there is still only one bike I'm interested in," Walksler said. "Would you sell it?"

"Well, we might," said the son.

Walksler offered $15,000 cash, but the son told him his dad had been offered that much for the bike 15 or 20 years earlier. "At least that set a platform for the value," Walksler said.

While he had been touring the father's parts all day long, he had discovered a cam cover for a 1936 Knucklehead, a rare part he needed. "The son counter-offered that he would sell the orange bike for $20,000. I said it was a deal if he would throw in the cam cover. He agreed and we loaded it onto the trailer."

They had to cut the bike from the ceiling, where it had been hanging from a chain for at least 40 years.

"So I'm driving home," Walksler said, thinking, 'what the hell did I just buy?'"

As he was driving, his mind was centered on the J-type motor, which had a rear-mounted magneto and the front-mounted timer cable. He began to think that perhaps it in fact may have had a front-mounted magneto.

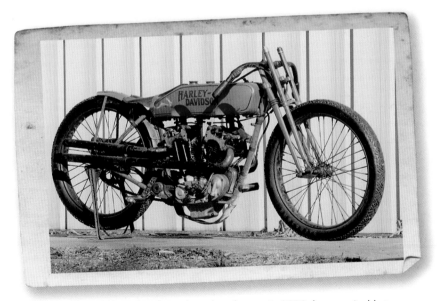

Walksler had heard about this elusive board track racer in 1990, but wasn't able to call it his own for more than 20 years. It had been hanging from the ceiling of a Kansas farmhouse, above the freezer, in the previous owner's pantry. *Brad Bowling*

"I pulled over and got out my tape measure," he said. "I measured the motor mount, three and a half inches, center to center. Then I called my son Matt back at the museum. He measured the motor mount on the factory DAH hill-climber. Three and a half inches. I knew exactly which engine fit that frame."

According to Walksler, the Harley factory built 20 or so hill-climbers between 1929 and 1934. Four years earlier, Walksler had heard about a DAH (Designated As Harley) engine for sale in Seattle, but it was so far away that he took a pass on it. Nashville-based collector Somer Hooker wound up buying the engine, which was mounted on a homemade frame. Hooker sold the engine to John Parham, who owns the National Motorcycle Museum. Walksler took a look at the engine at the time and noticed that it was different from any of the other 20 DAH motors he had seen; it had four exhaust pipes, meaning it was a four-port engine, with pushrod covers and an oiling system, none of which was standard for a DAH.

Walksler recorded the motor details in his brain. But when he successfully purchased the orange racing frame, he realized that Parham's engine was probably the correct engine for his frame. "I called Parham," he said. "I told him what I had discovered and found out that he paid between $30,000 to $40,000 for the motor. Afterward, he sent me an e-mail suggesting a trade, but I never received it! In this business, the Internet is both a blessing and a curse. A month later I saw John at a swap meet and he said, 'Well, what do you think of my deal?' I said, 'What deal?'"

"We both had a good laugh over that. It turns out that John and I traded—the engine for two Harley-powered midget race cars. One had a J-motor, and the other had a Knucklehead."

The happy ending to the story is that Walksler was able to reunite a one-of-a-kind frame with a one-of-a-kind motor. Still, nobody knows how the bike wound up in Kansas and the engine in Seattle. It is amazing that these two components, separated more than a half-century earlier, were reunited.

Walksler races the bike in vintage events these days, but in August 2010 he also entered it in the Pebble Beach Concours. While at Pebble, he was interviewed by another well-known collector: Jay Leno. After a friendly chat that was featured on www.jaylenosgarage.com, Leno offered a nice plug to Walksler's museum.

"The Wheels Through Time Museum in Maggie Valley, North Carolina, is one of the best in the world, and you must visit it," said Leno.

If you want to see the ultimate collection of vintage bikes, go visit Dale Walksler in Maggie Valley and ask him about his bikes.

LICENSE AND REGISTRATION, PLEASE...

Raymond Miller of North Carolina didn't think too much about the history of the '41 Knucklehead barn-find he had purchased for restoration. It was just a good, solid old bike that didn't seem very special at first. But when he began its disassembly, he started to look seriously at the serial numbers.

"The engine looked brand new," said Miller. "Whoever put it up as a drag racer evidently took extremely good care of or didn't use it very much. It had drag fuel carburetors and a lot of the parts were lightened as much as they could."

The bike was purchased along with a score of other motorcycle components, mostly Harley-Davidson. Eventually Miller conducted a reference check on the engine serial numbers and discovered it was a police engine. It was an easy decision—he would restore it as a police bike.

It would be the fourth police motorcycle that Miller would restore. It was a natural extension of his interest in early police AM and FM radio

Raymond Miller didn't think much about the '41 Knucklehead he had recently purchased along with a pile of spare Harley parts. He thought it might have been an old drag bike because it had drag carburetors and a bunch of lightened parts. *Raymond Miller*

Miller had long been fascinated with police AM and FM radios. Mounted below the fire extinguisher is one-half of an AM radio that was used on pre–World War II police bikes. These radios could only receive, but not transmit. Pre-war AM radios were manufactured by the American division of the German Bosch Corporation, which was located in Springfield, Massachusetts, home of Indian Motorcycles. *Tom Cotter*

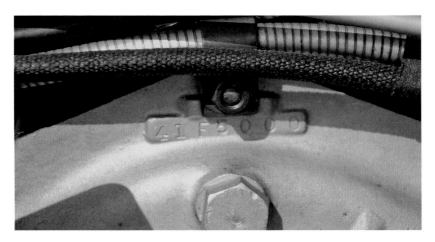

When he noticed the serial number on the block, though, he realized that when this bike left the factory, it had likely been a police model, so he spent several years chasing down police-specific pieces. *Tom Cotter*

Hard to believe this first aid kit, manufactured in Newark, New Jersey, is seven decades old. It still contains the original bandages, iodine, and wraps. *Tom Cotter*

This automotive-type voltage regulator (upper-left) and generator were able to produce up to 24 volts, twice that of a passenger Harley. Notice the wheel-driven siren to the rear. *Tom Cotter*

transmission (AM is short for Amplitude Modulation and FM stands for Frequency Modulation). "In 1941, police bikes had radio equipment mounted on both sides of the bike," he said. "One side was for the power supply and the other was for the AM receiver. In those days, police officers could only listen, not talk back because there was no FM band. All they had was an AM receiver."

According to Miller, before World War II, police officers had to be within range of an AM transmitter because the signal didn't travel far and it was noisy. In order to suppress static and electronic "noise" from interfering with AM reception, early police bikes were equipped with shielded spark plug wires and shielded voltage regulator cables. But significant noise was still produced.

In North Carolina, where Miller lives, there were only four police transmitters across the state: in Asheville, Salisbury, Goldsboro, and Raleigh. "So if you worked in range of one of those stations, you could hear what they were saying," he said. But you couldn't call for backup. You were on your own. You had to do what the dispatcher told you to do and that was it.

"Then, in 1938, from what I understand, five highway patrol cars in Connecticut were equipped with experimental FM two-way radios. The United States Army sent a major up there to check them out. He borrowed two of them and as a result, all our tanks in World War II were equipped with FM equipment."

Miller is not sure if North Carolina police officers were required to be right-handed, but this authentic ticket pad holder was designed to mount only on the right side of the handlebars. *Tom Cotter*

Miller explained that police radio technology gave the United States a communications advantage over the German army. "Rommel [only] had AM frequency, so we could talk, but he couldn't," he said. "So after the war, everything went to FM."

Miller started to purchase police radio equipment years ago, well before other collectors caught on to their unique features. He attended flea markets and purchased radios and related equipment. "At a flea market somebody would walk by and tell me they saw an unusual rack for sale, and I would pick it up because I knew it was a radio rack," he said. He picked up handlebar-mounted speakers that included a volume control, and the radio on his '41 Harley was manufactured by American Bosch in Springfield, Massachusetts, home of Indian Motorcycles.

Miller also bought other police-specific bike accessories, such as first aid kits. His 1941 Harley has a brand-new first aid kit that Miller discovered in a flea market years earlier. This one includes iodine, bandages, and wrap, untouched after more than 70 years.

Miller's '41 Knucklehead is a kick-start bike.

Police bikes had a special generator with an "R" stamped into the case after the serial number. Because of the extra demands of a police motorcycle, the generator produced 20 or 24 amps, about twice the amount of a standard unit. The radio battery alone required 6 amps.

Miller's bike has the required fire extinguisher, which, when new, was filled with carbon tetrachloride, which is poison. "The extinguisher is empty now, because the contents have been outlawed," Miller said. "It's an accumulative poison, which could never be cleansed from your body." The fire may not kill you, but the poison would.

The bike's siren is driven off the rear wheel, similar to generator-driven headlights on 1960s bicycles. If the siren was left against the bike's wheel, the noise would be constant. Only taking the siren on and off the wheel would modulate the sound to the more traditional police siren we hear today.

Miller also found a handlebar-mounted writing pad holder for writing tickets. He notes, though, that it was only functional for right-handed officers.

Police motorcycles had special speedometers. These had a function that allowed an officer to lock in the speed of the vehicle in pursuit to show as evidence to the violating driver. And as with all Harley speedometers, it had a turn-back odometer.

Finally, the red police lights did not flash on 1941 police bikes, but stayed on constantly.

Except for the engine, everything else—brakes, crash bars, fenders, gas tank, taillights, wheels, and tires—were standard Harley-Davidson issue.

Miller mentioned that Harley manufactured about 150 police-special engines in 1941. He said they were low-compression, high-horsepower F-series engines of 74 cubic inches.

As Miller was restoring his Knucklehead, he found an unopened, original can of low-satin silver police paint, used by officers in North Carolina.

"I opened it, but it was so old that it had turned to shellac," he said. "Harley added aluminum powder to shellac and called it Police Silver. So I basically did the same thing."

Miller regrets not taking as-found photos of his bike prior to restoration, but plenty have been taken of the bike since the restoration was complete.

His friend Dicky Panuski, who actually purchased another of Miller's police bike restorations, said this is a special bike. "When most people restore this type of bike, they usually buy new sheet metal and reproduction parts," Panuski said. "Even though this bike was just a pile of parts when Raymond bought it, he worked with all the original parts. This bike has all original fenders and gas tank."

The incredible restoration has been driven less than two miles since completion, but it has appeared at a number of shows. Miller's '41 Knucklehead has received the highest award the Antique Automobile Club of America (AACA) can award a motorcycle, a Senior First. He turned down a $50K offer for the bike.

"I really need to ride it about 100 miles or so, because it probably needs some adjustments," he concludes.

THE HEFFRON TRIUMPH
by Larry Edsall

For Tom Heffron, the bike bug bit early. "When I was a kid, there was a guy up the street—this was probably in 1975—who had a Harley Sportster, and the next year he bought a Norton Commando, and I think I remember a 1969 Triumph Bonneville before those," Heffron said.

Heffron got his first motorcycle in 1979, and five years later moved up to what he considered his dream ride—his own Sportster. "I always wanted a Sportster," he said. "In 1984 I bought an '82 that had been sitting on the showroom floor for two years." The Sportster became his daily rider and also was used for long-distance touring in the upper Midwest, where Heffron was an art director for a Twin Cities–area book publisher.

But then another bike bug bit Heffron. "The vintage bike bug," he said.

In 1989, a friend of Heffron's bought a '69 Bonneville and converted it to a chopper-style ride. Heffron became intrigued by the thought of a vintage bike, but his goal wasn't to customize or to modernize such a ride, but to either keep it or to return it to its original specification. He even knew which bike he wanted.

A chance conversation with a female police officer, who mentioned that her husband had a Triumph motorcycle in the garage, yielded Tom Heffron this primo 1970 Trophy T100C. For $700, he got this very straight and correct, honest-to-God, Jacaranda Purple bike.
Tom Heffron

137

In the mid-1980s, Heffron enjoyed a record album by the British group Prefab Sprout. The group's second album was sold in the United States under the title "Two Wheels Good." The original release name in England had been "Steve McQueen," but the family of the late actor and car, and motorcycle racer wouldn't let his name be used that way in the United States, even though the band had named its album in tribute to McQueen, and had posed on the album cover with a mid-1960s Triumph.

"I'd become enamored by that bike," Heffron said. So in 1990, he set out to buy such a bike. He didn't have to wait long.

"In April, a buddy and I went to a bike auction, and I jumped the gun and bought a '73 Bonneville," Heffron said, who discovered when he got the bike home that it really wasn't what he thought it was; it had been cobbled together from several bikes.

Stunned but undaunted, Heffron set out again and found another vintage bike. It was only $600, but again, it wasn't the bike he was pursuing. "I got those two bikes, but I kept thinking that they're fine, but there was something about them that was not capturing the bike I had in mind," Heffron said.

Although the bikes didn't meet his expectations, he decided he needed to get them registered so he could ride them. "I called the local police department in the village of North Hudson," said Heffron, who lived east of the Twin Cities in the small Wisconsin village on the bluff above the picturesque St. Croix River. At the time, the registration process for a used vehicle began with a visit from a local deputy, to verify the vehicle's identification numbers.

"A deputy pulled up, came to the garage, and looked at the bikes and was jotting down the numbers and she says, 'Ah, a Triumph, that's interesting,'" Heffron recalled.

"Why's that?" he asked.

"My husband has one in the garage," she responded. "I'm trying to get him to sell it. Any chance you might be interested in another one?"

Heffron said he'd like to see the bike. He jumped onto his Sportster and followed the squad car to the officer's house, just five blocks from Heffron's home. "She pulled into the driveway and I can see the garage door going up," Heffron said. "She had not described the bike in any way. She didn't know what model it was. But the first thing I saw as the door lifted was the high pipe, which looked just like the bike on the record cover. I just flipped."

The bike was a 1970 Triumph Trophy T100C, a 500cc Scrambler with side pipe.

"Are you interested?" the deputy asked.

"Absolutely!" Heffron said.

The deputy's husband was out of town and wouldn't be back for several days. Heffron took the phone number, waited until he returned home, and called.

"Oh, there's another guy interested," Heffron was told, "but he wants to make a hill-climber out of it and I don't want to see it get hacked up."

"I bet I hadn't seen such a stock Triumph in 15 to 20 years," Heffron said. "It was all original and all there, the original high pipes, the perfect seat cover, the Jacaranda Purple paint. There was honest wear, but not bad for a 20-year-old Triumph."

"There's no way I'm going to hack it up," Heffron told the deputy's husband. "I'm going to leave it bone stock." The deputy's husband also wanted the bike to remain unchanged, admitted "there's a small wiring problem," and finally asked for $700.

"I could do $700," Heffron said.

He got the bike and within half an hour had it running—the electrical problem was nothing more than a broken wire.

The next day, Heffron's phone rang. It was the deputy, and she sounded excited.

"She said, 'We have something for you, for your bike, and you have to come over and get it!'" Heffron wondered what it could be—the bike seemed complete. Even the original tool box and owner's manual had come with it.

He rode to the deputy's house, where the couple presented him with a small threaded plastic knob that held the tool box to one of the bike's side covers but at some point had been removed and become separated from the bike. She'd found the knob in her kitchen junk drawer. It wasn't much, but it added to the completeness of the bike, made it more whole.

Two Wheels Good. Third Time Charm.

MY FIRST ANTIQUE HARLEY(S)
by Buzz Kanter

I had been riding mini bikes since I was a kid and bought my first motorcycle in college. It was a beat-up old Honda 305cc Superhawk. It didn't take long before I was trading up to ever larger and faster performance motorcycles for the street and race-track. After years of buying and selling perhaps a hundred motorcycles from the 1960s, 1970s, and 1980s I eventually purchased my first antique motorcycle, a World War II–era British BSA M20, in 1986. Back then I never even considered riding a Harley. All that changed in the early 1990s when I got my first Sportster and purchased a small magazine called *American Iron Magazine* that was about to go out of business.

Over the years I have learned there are many wonderful old motorcycles stashed away and out of sight, often ignored by owners and their families. Occasionally these old treasures are for sale and others might be under the right conditions. Some owners have grossly inflated ideas of what they are worth and often do not even know what they are, and others just want to get rid of them to clean up the place. When tracking down a lead for an old bike, you never know where it might take you. So my advice is to do your homework and be prepared to move quickly—either to buy on the spot or to walk away from a bad deal.

A chance conversation at a HOG ride about "a couple of really old Harleys or Indians" at a nearby gas station soon had collector Kanter investigating. Lucky for him, the bike didn't turn out to be a "Honda with Harley decals," but a 1929 and a 1924 Harley JDCA. *Buzz Kanter*

One evening I was out riding my Sportster with some local HOG (Harley Owners Group) members when one of them asked if I had seen the two old motorcycles for sale at a gas station two towns over. I hear a lot of these stories and they usually turn out to be nothing, but I always try to investigate, as you never know where they might lead. And sometimes that's all part of the fun. I asked for more information. He said they were "real old" and thought they were Harleys or Indians. That got my attention. All too often an "antique motorcycle" turns out to be a 1960s Honda with Harley stickers on the gas tank or worse. But I'd hate not to follow up on a lead that might be the real deal.

A few days later I stopped by the gas station to ask about the bikes and was told they had been moved and it was their owner's day off. The manager there told me they were "real old Harleys, like from World War I." I thanked him and left my name and phone number for the seller to call me. I didn't hear from him, so I visited again two weeks later. The seller was out again. After that, it slipped my mind for two or three months. The next time I was in the area, I visited the gas station and was told the bikes were still for sale but the seller no longer worked there. He was building a new car wash a few miles away. It was a beautiful day so I rode over to the new car wash construction site and finally met the owner of the old Harleys.

I told him I had heard he had some old Harleys for sale. He said they were both from the 1920s, in great condition, and very rare and valuable. I told him I was interested in buying one or both of them. I followed him over to a small cramped basement storage space a few miles away. We had to move an old mildewing mattress and lots of cardboard boxes full of junk, but under it all I could see a pair of dirty, rusty old Harleys leaning against the basement wall. My heartbeat quickened as I climbed over all the junk to have a better look.

As is often the case, the seller—who actually knew very little about either of the bikes, a 1924 and a 1929 Harley V-twin—claimed they were worth more than twice what I valued them at. I tried to educate him a little about those particular machines and how I came up with my value of less than half his. He was pretty steadfast on his price and said he might drop 10 percent if I bought them both. I politely thanked him for his time and gave him my name and contact info. I said I'd appreciate hearing from him if he would consider my offer and I wished him luck with his new car wash. In my dealings I am always honest and try to be polite as you never know where it might lead. As I got in my car to drive away I half expected him to call me back and renegotiate, but no.

About two months later I got a call from the seller. He was running short of money to complete the building for his car wash and wanted to see if we could do a deal. We pulled the old Harleys out of the basement to better look them

Kanter displayed the '24 for several years at his *American Iron Magazine* offices and at the Wheels Through Time Museum in North Carolina. All were amazed at how original and authentic the bike remained after more than seven decades. *Buzz Kanter*

over. I told him my last offer was still good for either of the bikes and he could choose which one. After some negotiations I increased my offer 10 percent and we agreed I'd pay for and pick up the 1924 Harley in a few days.

This was the oldest and most expensive motorcycle I had ever purchased, and I was pretty excited. I thought a lot about this deal and the second old Harley. I wondered when I'd find another deal like this. So I called the seller and offered to buy them both at twice my original offer for either one. He accepted my offer and we did the deal.

Once I got the two bikes home I looked them over more carefully. The '29 Harley was a mess, with bad repaint and missing a lot of important parts. I decided to do a total nuts and bolts ground-up restoration on it. But to me, the all-original '24 Harley JDCA suffering from a stuck engine that would not turn over looked perfect just as I bought it. I pumped up the original tires to make it easier to roll around, did a quick and simple cleaning, and displayed it "as found" in the *American Iron Magazine* offices for several years. And that's where it sat until my pal Dale Walksler of the Wheels Through Time Museum called and, sight unseen, offered to go through the bike and get it running for me.

When the truck carried the old Harley down to Dale's museum in Maggie Valley, North Carolina, he called to tell me he was blown away by how complete, original, and correct it was. He was pretty excited by the bike

Dale Walksler from Wheels Through Time diagnosed a bent valve in the engine. He replaced that, installed a new battery, and tuned the carb, and Kanter's bike was purring like a kitten. *Buzz Kanter*

Not a restoration queen, nearly every nut and bolt on Kanter's Harley that were installed and tightened by the factory mechanics are still in place today. *Buzz Kanter*

and told me he was looking forward to hearing it run—something it had not done in decades.

Three or four days later Dale called me and said he wanted me to hear something. I listened and heard him kick-start a motorcycle and rev it up a bit. I asked what it was and he laughed and told me it was my '24 Harley. It sounded strong and even as he revved it up and down for me to hear.

A few days earlier, Dale got it into his workshop and soaked the engine with penetrating oil to see if he could free up whatever was stuck. He couldn't. So he started digging into the top end and discovered a bent valve jammed in place. He found an NOS replacement valve and pocket in his seemingly endless collection of antique motorcycle parts, and installed it in my Harley. Voila! The engine spun over with relative ease. He cleaned and adjusted the carb, installed a 6-volt battery, poured fresh oil in the engine and transmission, and finally added some gas. Then he began kicking it over. Dale is the Mechanical Maestro when it comes to bringing old motorcycles back to life, and this time was no exception.

It was a matter of minutes before Dale got the bike to fire and run, but only for a second or two before it died. This happened several times before he could get the bike to rev properly. Then, while throttling up and down, smoke began bellowing from the engine and several flaming acorns flew out of the exhaust tip. The acorns had blocked the muffler from letting the exhaust escape and that's why

Kanter (pictured), publisher of *American Iron Magazine*, plans to ride his '24 Harley barn-find on the 2013 Cannonball cross-country rally. *Buzz Kanter*

the bike kept stalling out. Once the bike got going, it heated up the acorns, and to Dale's surprise and delight, one hard throttle twist popped them out.

Once he got the old Harley running, there wasn't a lot more for Dale to do to get the bike sorted and back on the road. Leaving all the original paint parts on the bike, he replaced the rotting old tires, changed the burned-out taillight, and spliced less than three inches of new wire into the original harness. That was about it.

Since then, I have done little to this bike other than typical maintenance issues. I have ridden it several thousand street miles, including a few parade laps of the Mid-Ohio racetrack, and winning first place on the USCRA's Pewter Run (United States Classic Racing Association) timed endurance ride in New Hampshire. My '24 barn-find Harley was the oldest bike in the annual Pewter Run that year, making the overall win that much more exciting for me.

When he is not searching for, restoring, or riding his classic motorcycles, Buzz Kanter is the publisher of American Iron Magazine, *the best-selling Harley magazine in the world, and also publisher of* Motorcycle Bagger *and* RoadBike *magazines. Find him online at www.caimag.com.*

THE BARN-FIND BULTACO
by Larry Edsall

For Ken Kelly, obtaining the bike was the easy part. Finding out just what he had, well, that was another story.

Ken and his brother, Al, are known in New Jersey as the Crapoholic Brothers, siblings eager to secure old motorcycles and motorcycle parts for their own and for others' restoration and preservation efforts.

Ken explains that Al came up with the term "crapoholic" long before being a "picker" was fashionable. "We always went hunting for signs and things, but primarily for motorcycles," Ken said of the Kellys' lifelong hobby.

Al Kelly's nearly 20-year quest to gain access to "The Jurassic Junkyard" and Ken's role in the eventual and dramatic rescue of 1930 and 1944 Indians, a 1957 Harley-Davidson, and a 1946 Harley "Knucklehead" engine was the opening story in *The Vincent in the Barn*.

Such "crimes of persistence" sometimes pay off in unexpected ways. For example, because of the brothers' reputation, Al Kelly was called one day in 2005 by someone who had just obtained several old motorcycles while cleaning out the remains of an estate sale.

"Al went to see the bikes and found they were exceptionally dirty and grungy, covered with years of soot and grime," Ken said. "The seller really didn't know very much about them [they were European bikes, not the American bikes the Kellys usually pursued], but the price seemed right so Al bought them."

But after he got the bikes home, Al realized they really didn't "float his boat," so he asked Ken if he might be interested in part of the cache, which included an old BSA Goldstar and a couple of Bultacos. "I was never particularly hot for British iron, but having roots in off-road riding from a very early age, I always had a lot of respect for Bultacos, so I went to check out the bikes," Ken said.

"I was surprised to see that they looked like small, single-cylinder, early crotch rockets," he added. "They had long tanks, bubble-butt seats, and clip-on handlebars. One of them had lights and old plates on it and was set up for road use, but the other was obviously built specifically for competition and had the remains of some Bonneville decals left on the fuel tank.

"I'll have to admit, up to that point, I never even knew Bultaco made anything but off-road bikes. I found myself strangely attracted to the funny-looking little racer, so a deal was made and the Bultacos were loaded up and were once again on their way to a new home."

Bultaco was founded in 1958 by Francisco Xavier "Paco" Bulto, who joined two others, including his brother-in-law, in launching the Montesa motorcycle company in Barcelona at the conclusion of World War II. Bulto ventured out on his own in part because others in the company wanted to stop motorsports activities, which Bulto managed. Bultaco, named by combining the *Bult* from *Bulto* with the *aco* from *Paco*, became one of the most successful off-pavement racing bike producers in motorcycling history.

"I always like to start on a new project with a basic cleaning, as there is no better way to get a thorough look and evaluation of the details of a bike than to spend the better part of a day bustin' knuckles scrubbing every square inch of it," Ken Kelly said.

"This bike had to rank up there with the worst of them [in crustiness]," he added. "There were so many layers of built-up soot and grunge, it took every type of poking device, scraper, and brush I owned to remove the years of crud from within all the nooks and crannies, being careful not to harm the underlying surfaces as I went."

Kelly compared the project more to an archaeological dig than a motorcycle cleaning as he transformed the bike into what he calls "a 15-footer, meaning it looked pretty decent from 15 or more feet away."

This Bultaco was one of several estate-sale bikes that the Kelly Brothers picked up. Finding old "Bonneville" decals on the bike, Ken Kelly discovered that this bike had been set up by the factory to run speed records. The bike is currently on display at the Motorcyclepedia Museum in Newburgh, New York. *Ken Kelly*

This is the bike as it competed at the Bonneville Salt Flats in Utah, in 1974. Bultaco motorcycles are known mostly for their off-road motorcycles; the speed record bike takes even the most serious collectors by surprise. *Ken Kelly*

While the bike still was dripping rust penetrate, Kelly started documenting serial numbers on the engine and frame, recording missing pieces—which included the carburetor, exhaust system, gauges, and fairings—and began making detailed photographs.

He then started doing research on the bike, chancing upon a small and forgotten paperback book, *Racing Motorcycles*, in his library. The book had been written in Italy, but Kelly had an English translation. In the section of the book on Spanish motorcycles, Kelly found a bike that looked a lot like his, a Bultaco 250 TSS air-cooled racer. Additional research on the Internet took him to the website for Hugh's Bultaco in upstate New York. He discovered that what he had was a model 29, a 350 TSS air-cooled factory racer built in 1969 and 1970.

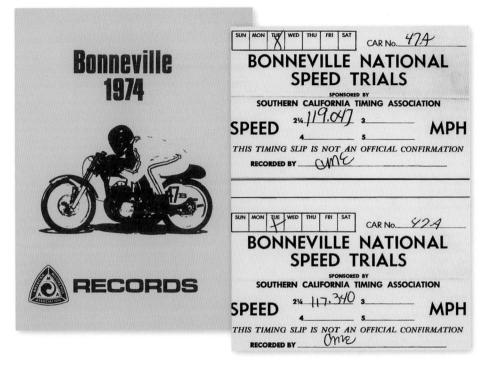

Kelly's Bultaco came with a Bonneville logbook that listed two of the bike's runs in 1974—117.340 and 119.047 mph. *Ken Kelly*

Kelly contacted Don McCullough of the TSS Owners Registry. "I sent off an email to Don, who responded quickly as he was the builder of the registry and was excited to hear the news that the long-missing No. 54 [bike] was found," Kelly said. "He filled me in on the production details, explaining there were 57 total units built, with 52 in 1969 and just five in 1970. My serial number of 54 makes it one of the five bikes built in 1970. The 350 was the biggest and the last of the TSS line.

"Now I'm getting excited," Kelly said. And things soon would become even more exciting.

"Along with starting a search for missing components, I started my journey of seeing if there was any significance to the remnants of Bonneville decals left on the side of the fuel tank," Kelly said.

The secretary of the Southern California Timing Association that sanctioned speed runs on the Utah salt flats told Kelly that records were kept by rider name and vehicle entry registration number, neither of which Kelly knew.

"It wasn't looking good at this point, but I wasn't ready to throw in the towel just yet," Kelly said, who asked the secretary if there might be anyone else who might be of help. She suggested he contact Jim "J. D." Tone, a dry lakes racer and SCTA records certification official and historian.

Tone repeated what the club's secretary had said, and added that at the time the bike was racing, its 350cc engine made it eligible for some two dozen competition divisions. But Tone said he'd do what he could, adding, however, that Kelly should be low on expectations and long on patience.

"To my surprise, J. D. got back to me. He did find some results for the 1973 and 1974 for a Bultaco 350, and the driver was from New Jersey!" Kelly said. Nonetheless, "he was reluctant to give me any more information at the time. He said there were many people who re-create famous racing vehicles and coerce people like him to provide information to support their fabricated provenance."

Tone needed more information, and Kelly finally was able to track down the name of the estate where the bikes had been found. Tone confirmed the match and shared information including copies of timing sheets verifying the bike had set records in 1973 and 1974.

"A small piece of Bonneville and Bultaco history was preserved," Kelly said. "It was especially sweet to see the lone Bultaco listed among the surrounding 'Japanese invasion' in those early '70s records."

As happy as he was for confirmation of his bike's history, Kelly said he was even more disappointed not to have the bike's front fairing with its Bonneville entry numbers.

Three years passed, and Al Kelly received a telephone call from a lawyer friend who had run into a former acquaintance of the estate's owner, who mentioned there was an attic crawl space above the house's kitchen that had been used for storage. It had yet to be entered, and the estate was looking for someone to get rid of whatever might be up there. "I didn't want to get my hopes up, but I could hardly stand the suspense," Ken said, "and quickly volunteered to help clear the attic and haul away its contents."

And what did he find?

In addition to six more dismantled motorcycles, "the missing original racing exhaust system along with the original wind fairing, complete with Bonneville numbers and safety inspection decals, were pulled out of their dark, dusty tomb and into the light of day once again," he reported.

Later, Kelly learned that the Bultaco's original oval-shaped Bonneville number plates were hanging on the wall in the basement of a friend who had bought some of the other bikes in the original cache from Al Kelly.

Finally back to its Bonneville condition, Ken Kelly offered his Bultaco on loan through 2012 as part of the Antique Motorcycle Foundation's "Fast

From the Past" racing bike exhibit at the new Motorcyclepedia Museum in Newburgh, New York.

"Often the true measure of the treasure is not recognized when first found," Ken Kelly said, "but is only made known as the remaining pieces are added and the puzzle is completed.

"And as in the case of the odd little bubble-butt Bultaco, many times the history of the bike and its journeys with its owners are as much or more of a treasure than the motorcycle itself."

CHAPTER FOUR

The Long Haul

ANOTHER BLACK BEAST RETURNS TO THE ROAD
by Denny Cornett III

The story of how I came to own a 1952 Vincent Black Shadow Series C really starts with my father, who is also named Denver (Denny) Cornett.

Dad was an imported car dealer back in the 1950s in Louisville, Kentucky. He had always been involved in the sports car world, having driven in the first Watkins Glen Grand Prix in 1948. (In fact, he was the original owner of a 1952 Cunningham C-3 coupe that is today in the collection of Tom Cotter, this book's author.)

While selling Jaguars one year, he took a Vincent Black Shadow in trade. He rode it a short time but didn't resell it because he thought it was too fast for the general public to handle. Fortunately, after a month, the bike's previous owner returned the Jaguar and wanted the Vincent back. So I had heard all about this mythical Vincent motorcycle, had seen a few at Vintage Motorcycle Days at Mid-Ohio, and decided I would own one someday.

I was most attracted to the Series C Black Shadow, which was introduced in 1949 with a 998cc overhead valve V-twin that produced 55 horsepower. Not only was the engine amazingly powerful and reliable for the time, but every aspect of the Vincent was innovative and forward-thinking. The frame, for example, had no front down tube; the powerplant doubled as a stressed member, which allowed engineers to increase the angle of the twin's "V" to 50 degrees for better cooling and torque.

From the factory, a Black Shadow only weighed 460 pounds and could top 125 miles per hour. They were the superbikes of their day.

In fact, it was those innovations that put the company out of business in 1955. Advertised as "the makers of the world's fastest motorcycles," Vincent was always a shoestring operation where engineering and speed were more important than profit. The hour-long documentary about the Vincent legend, titled *Chasing Shadows*, suggests that the company's goal was not to make money. Mission accomplished!

Many years passed and in 2002, I had saved enough money to realize my dream of Black Shadow ownership—and received my wife's blessing—when an ad appeared on www.thevincent.com for a '52 Series C, the exact model I desired. Luckily enough, it was just outside Columbus, Ohio, which was close enough for me to inspect it personally. These bikes were usually showing up overseas or on the west coast, which meant someone else snatched them up before I could get there. I hooked up my father's huge car trailer and headed to Ohio.

An exotic car mechanic named Gregory Jelkin was selling the Black Shadow because he was more interested in Moto Guzzis and other Italian rides than British bikes. Jelkin gave me the unusual history of this particular Vincent.

Creator Phil Vincent was obsessed with building his motorcycles as small and light as possible, in order to take maximum advantage of his powerful V-twin engines. With a rudimentary understanding of aerodynamics, he knew that getting the rider out of the airstream would aid acceleration and increase top speed. This profile shot of Denny Cornett's '52 Black Shadow illustrates this design philosophy.

Its first owner was a bridge builder in West Virginia who had been killed on the job shortly after buying the bike. His best friend bought it and rode it about 100 miles, only to mothball it for storage when it was still only a few years old. Forty-plus years later, around 1999, Jelkin was helping the Vincent's somewhat eccentric owner pull a Triumph motorcycle out of his shed when he noticed the Black Shadow in the back covered in drywall. Jelkin suggested they pull the Vincent out instead.

In spite of the care given its storage in the 1950s, time had not been kind to the Series C. Its battery had exploded at some point, and acid had eaten away some of the back fender and pipes. All of the rubber had rotted, and it was clear there were some wiring issues.

The bike had been hit at some point before its shed life by a big 1950s car, which explained the bent rear frame and bumper-shaped indention in the engine's fins. The forward carburetor had been substituted with an older unit, and one of the covers had been replaced. It had sustained quite a bit of damage to only have traveled 7,900 miles in its life.

Jelkin got the Vincent to turn over, and he knew from his research that such a machine was quite valuable. He was surprised when the owner said he could haul it away for free.

(According to Jelkin, this guy had several highly collectible vehicles on his property. There was a pre-war Mercedes race car and what turned out to be one of the earliest Harley-Davidsons ever built. That Harley is now on display in the company's museum in Milwaukee.)

Jelkin worked on the Vincent in his shop, making basic repairs such as replacing the muffler, wiring, and fenders. He kept it for a short while before posting it for sale on the Vincent website, home to hardcore Vincent owners and restorers.

I was lucky I saw the ad right away and lived so close by, or someone else surely would have grabbed it. I knew this was my chance to own a Vincent.

I was drawn to the fact that it had not been used up like a lot of 50-year-old motorcycles. So many of those were ridden hard, broken, and put away, but Jelkin's Vincent—despite the damage—could easily be restored to driving condition. I could see a lot of problems, such as a floppy kick start, the flaking black engine paint, and overall tatty condition, but I knew those were minor fixes compared to what I had seen on other bikes.

Vincent motorcycles were among the first to successfully use the engine and gearbox as integral parts of the frame. In fact, there isn't much frame to speak of, leading enthusiasts to nickname the Vincent Series B and Series C the "boneless wonders."

Even the Black Shadow's engine had an evil dark look about it. Reasons given for painting the case black range from aiding heat dissipation to preventing rust.

Jelkin had a lot of papers and manuals, which I knew would be otherwise difficult to find, so we negotiated a $27,000 price. This was right about the time that Vincent values were taking off, and I knew they would never get any cheaper.

I am lucky that my hometown of Louisville has a resident Vincent aficionado named Sid Biberman. Everybody knows him as simply "Big Sid." Sid is a master restorer of Vincents and considered an authority on the subject: Vincent designer Phil Irving has stated that Sid's restorations are nearly identical to what the Stevenage, England, factory produced.

I got the bike running but wanted Sid to assess it. It wasn't very pretty during that period, and scuttled down the road like a sand crab because of the bent frame, but I put a couple of hundred miles on it before taking it to Sid. I did not need it to be concours ready; I just wanted Sid's input and help to make it better.

Today, my Vincent still has fewer than 10,000 miles on it, and it's a blast to ride. I love just looking at it—even the engine is beautiful. There is a mystique about owning one of these bikes. Having one allows you to hang out with some pretty cool people sometimes, like Jay Leno.

The Vincent HRD Owners Club (www.voc.uk.com) was founded in 1948 and today has 2,500 members in 30 United Kingdom regions and 27 overseas regions. Its VOC Spares Co. has been reproducing Vincent parts since 1975 and, in 2006, the club created a Black Shadow entirely from new parts to show the completeness of its inventory. I think that shows just how much people love these old bikes that Phil Vincent built, and it makes me proud to own a tiny bit of that history.

Popular culture has really done a lot to immortalize the Vincent. Hunter S. Thompson wrote about the Black Shadow on several occasions. He seemed to be afraid of them, describing them as black beasts whose sole purpose was to kill riders with their tremendous speed. In his book *Fear and Loathing in Las Vegas: A Savage Journey to the Heart of the American Dream*, Thompson claimed the Vincent would outrun an F-111 until the fighter jet got airborne. When writing about the awesome and frighteningly fast Ducati 900 for *Cycle World* magazine in 1995, the legendary gonzo journalist compared it to the Vincent Black Shadow.

ECLECTIC COLLECTOR

Finding a motorcycle is like finding a job or a girlfriend; the best opportunities materialize when you're not looking for one.

While amassing his varied, 100-strong motorcycle collection, Jamie Waters, of Brewster, New York, runs the gamut of great barn-find experiences.

Second-Choice 1947 Indian Chief

Waters was minding his own business, racing his vintage Cooper Three at Lime Rock Park in Connecticut in 2009. A seasoned vintage motorcycle roadracer, he had been attending his first Vintage Sports Car Club of America (VSCCA) event, and had enrolled in a driving school to get his sportscar-racing license. A VSCCA official who had been helping Waters that weekend later e-mailed him an ad that had appeared on the Jaguar Owner's Club forum. It listed an estate sale of a man who had been active in the Jaguar club.

Discovered on a Jaguar Owner's Forum, Jamie Waters purchased two vintage bikes from the estate of a recently deceased enthusiast. One was this 1947 Indian Chief, which Waters initially had no interest in because of the cheesy-looking whitewall tires, windshield, and studded saddlebags. *Jamie Waters*

158

"My VSCCA friend knew I liked old bikes, and thought I'd be interested in the sale. The ad got my attention for a couple of reasons," Waters said. "It listed that the man's family was clearing out the dad's stuff, which included an XK120 and a couple of old motorcycles: an Indian and a Harley."

Waters had seen these types of ads before. He'd travel to remote sales, only to find that the prize amounted to a rusty Kawasaki or Honda with no collector value. So he e-mailed the family and they sent him a few photos of the bikes.

He immediately noticed the Indian Chief, a terrific find for a collector. But the bike that excited Waters most was the 1931 Harley-Davidson DL, which had a rare 750cc high-compression side-valve engine. "I thought that would be a great project bike," Waters said. "It appeared to be all there, but was really rough around the edges. The Indian Chief, on the other hand, was nearly perfect. It had this peppermint-stick, barber-shop-quartet look to it. It was really jazzed up with studded saddlebags, a large Plexiglas windscreen, and whitewall tires. It just wasn't my thing."

Waters was normally into European roadracing bikes, and had only recently turned his attention to American machines. But the photos were enough to peak Waters' interest, so he traveled to the man's house just north of New York City. The bikes were in the basement, and it was obvious that they had not been moved in a few years. "The son was probably in his forties or fifties, and knew very little about the bikes," he said. "They simply weren't bike people and never caught the old man's bug."

The "old man" had been rather meticulous in his record-keeping, though, having kept all the registrations and other documents in a folder. Even though the bikes hadn't been ridden in years, their registrations had been current since the mid-1970s. "I inspected the motors and realized that the serial numbers on the engines and the frames matched on both the DL and the Chief."

Waters was also impressed with the man's workshop. "He had a beautiful hobby lathe and milling machine," he said. "Clearly this guy was detail-oriented and appreciated what he had. His tools were spotless and they all had a specific place."

Waters purchased the bikes and brought them home to his shop. He immediately spoke to a friend knowledgeable about Indians, who said there was a good market for the Indian Chief, and that it could sell for $12,000–15,000 as-is: not running, but complete, or about what he was paying for the pair of bikes.

"I was able to buy both bikes for that price, so I was basically getting the Harley for free if I could sell the Indian," he said.

He started tinkering with the Harley, but mostly ignored the Indian, which was in far better condition. When people visited his shop, it was the Indian that immediately caught their eyes. A friend had been bugging Waters about buying the Indian.

"He's pretty mechanically inclined, so I wound up selling him the bike, figuring he'd actually do something with it and that I'd still be able to see the bike often," said Waters. "He spent a couple of days fiddling with it, changed the fluids, checked the plugs and points, charged the battery and got it running. In the process of cleaning up the bike, he also removed the saddlebags and the windscreen. He sent me a video, and I thought to myself, 'I could have done that!' I had assumed it would have to come apart. I didn't know it would be that easy, or the bike would sound so sweet."

Meanwhile, Waters was becoming more and more frustrated with the Harley. And his remorse over selling the Indian was setting in, big time.

"So my friend gets the Indian running and he's farting around with it in his driveway, trying to come to terms with the controls," Waters said. "Indians have a foot clutch, a hand shift, the throttle is on the left side, and a timing advance/retard control on the right where the throttle is normally.

"But he just wasn't comfortable with the bike and he pranged the side of his Triumph TR-6. I think that kind of killed it for him. He called me only a month after I sold the Indian to him and said he was posting it on eBay."

The other bike was this 1931 Harley DL with a rare 750cc high-compression, side valve engine. This was the bike that Waters originally wanted to keep. *Jamie Waters*

After selling the Indian, regretting the decision, and buying it back, Waters removed the windshield and installed correct blackwall tires. Turns out this bike is a Bonneville model, with nine more horsepower than stock. It is now one of his favorite bikes. And the Harley was sold. *Jamie Waters*

Waters became frustrated with the Harley and depressed about the Indian—but still undecided on whether he should bid on it or not. Then the friend who originally consulted with him about the Indian urged Waters to buy the bike back.

"You know, that Chief was in a lot better condition than I thought it was," said the friend, after seeing the photos on eBay. "I don't think you should have gotten rid of it."

The listing noted that the carburetor had "BONN" cast into it, which Waters' friend said was a special race piece and worth good money on its own. At this point, the carburetor on the bike really didn't matter much to Waters. He simply knew he'd made a mistake in selling the bike and wanted it back.

But now, with six days left in the auction, bidding had started to skyrocket. The price of the bike had already climbed to $19,000. "I called my friend and told him I had made a horrible mistake," he said. "I asked if he would end the auction and sell me the bike back."

His friend pulled the bike off eBay, received a small premium for the work and money he had invested, and Waters again owned the Indian. He took the bike back into his shop and immediately replaced the whitewall tires. "Once I installed a set of period-correct, bias-ply blackwall tires, the bike was totally transformed," he said.

His Indian-guru friend came over the following weekend and the two looked over the bike in detail. His friend took special interest in the "BM" cast into the engine case, which Waters thought had stood for "battery/magneto." It turns out that it actually stood for "Bonneville Motor."

Only a handful of these Bonneville Indians were manufactured each year. The engines were high performance with a high-lift camshaft, special high-compression pistons, and magneto ignition. Installing the engines on street models allowed Indian to homologate (register for competition) the parts for their racing models. In that era, standard Indian Chiefs had 40 horsepower, but the Bonneville models had 49 horsepower, an increase of more than 20 percent.

"The bike has 43,000 miles on the odometer, and it's full of patina," said Waters. "The Indian Red paint is old, but it almost looks too good to be original. And the heavily worn seat fits like an old glove. It's a very comfortable bike to ride, with torque everywhere. It's the one that I ride on weekends most often. There is simply no pressure when you're on a bike like this. Nobody wants to race you, people pass with care, and cops don't look at you with suspicion."

And the '31 Harley he preferred when he purchased the pair?

"I sold it to a friend," he said. "I got $2,500 for it and haven't thought about it since."

Two Brothers' Rare Norton

Waters owns many motorcycles, but he's mostly into Nortons, specifically factory racers.

"I got into Nortons about 15 years ago," he said. "I had just moved to New York City and knew I wanted a British bike. As an analyst by trade, it was only natural for me to research my options. I focused on Triumphs, BSAs, and Nortons, but the deeper I got, the more obvious the choice became: Nortons. In fact, and perhaps naively, I couldn't believe that anyone even bought Triumphs. The frames are just awful in comparison. So I bought a 1971 Commando, which I still have. For a 40-year-old bike, the performance is incredible. It's now well sorted and will cruise at 85 miles per hour with no problems or vibration, thanks to its isolastic mounting of the engine, transmission, and swing arm."

The rarest Norton Waters owns is an ex-works, John Player monocoque racer. One of only four ever made, it is thought by former team manager Frank Perris to have won the 1973 Formula 750 TT race.

Bringing home the booty. Waters drove a Rider rental box truck from Connecticut to Minnesota, bought the Norton, strapped it into the box truck, and drove home with his new treasure. *Jamie Waters*

"I bought it from a couple of brothers in Minnesota, who bought it from the factory when it went bankrupt," said Waters. "It had been stored in a California warehouse all that time, and they paid about $4,500 for it, as I recall. Mine is the only original one left, the other three having been restored from bare frames, either as a result of fire or parting out by the team when they changed frame architecture from monocoque in 1973 to tubular space frame in 1974. Thankfully mine was sent to the United States after the 1973 season for Norton team rider Dave Aldana to give it one last go in the 1974 Daytona 200. After that, it stayed in the U.S., first in storage at Norton/Villiers/Triumph headquarters in California, then in the brothers' building around 1977."

These monocoque Norton racers are quite special. Their frames are made of two-ply, 22-gauge stainless steel sheet, and everything that bolts to it is fiberglass, aluminum, or magnesium. The frame is hand-welded of 600 individual pieces of stainless steel. The frame also had a ram airbox that ducted cold air from under the steering stem, up and over the engine, and into the carburetors.

This innovative frame, which bears striking resemblance to today's more contemporary design, contained the fuel and oil, and acted as a mount for the bodywork and an airbox for the carbs.

Because the fuel was stored below the carburetors, a fuel pump was required. Initially an automotive-type mechanical pump was mounted near the rear suspension swing-arm pivot, so that when the swing arm moved up and down, an arm moved the fuel pump, which pumped fuel into a header tank above the carburetors. It was all unique.

"The brothers knew what they had," he said. "It was still in as-raced condition, and once a year they rolled the engine over to keep it lubricated, and they changed the brake fluid. But they never started it. The bike sat for 29 years in the least secure conditions of any of the other monocoque bikes, but it's the only one to have survived undamaged all those years.

"I rented a Rider box truck and drove to Rochester, Minnesota, with a buddy to pick it up. The brothers, who lived near their shop, were terrific custodians of this bike. In their building, they had a couple of other choice Nortons, including an F-1 rotary."

Collectors heard rumors of the bike over the years, and had made offers. Waters, who had first contacted the brothers about the special Norton several years earlier, made an offer as well.

"They got back to me and said we have a deal," said Waters. "Obviously that meant I was the high bidder. I got the price down a bit more from there, but they were tough negotiators . . . and I wanted the bike! It's the centerpiece of my collection. It's one of the world's most historic racing bikes, it's in as-raced condition, and it has a bulletproof chain of ownership. The four JPN Norton monocoque bikes won 13 International races in all, during a very difficult period for four-stroke 750s."

Waters explained that in 1973 and 1974, two-stroke racing motorcycles were the hot ticket. "These 250 and 350, then 700 and 750cc two-strokes generated power with every revolution of the crank. So they were capable of producing almost twice the horsepower of an equivalently sized four-stroke engine, but with the additional benefit of substantially lighter weight," he said. "This produced about 76 horsepower at the crank and 67 horsepower at the rear wheel, while 750cc two-stroke competitors from the Japanese manufacturers realized up to 120 horsepower from the engines. Competing against Suzuki, Yamaha, and Kawasaki two-strokes, these Nortons were still capable of winning because of their superior handling and focus on low-drag aerodynamics.

"The brothers chose me because it was important to them who bought their bike—who would be the next caretaker. They still call to check on it once in a while."

Special Yamaha/Norton Racers

An eBay listing about five years ago got Waters' attention. It listed a 1974 Yamaha TZ250, which was a track-only, GP-based over-the-counter race bike. But what really got Waters' attention was that the auction not only included a large amount of spare parts, it also included a Norton race bike, although in parts.

The original owner had bought the bikes new and kept them until his death. A friend was selling them on behalf of the widow.

"She wanted the stuff sold in one lump. The items included technical notes, manuals, spares, receipts, and the original purchase documents from when he bought the Yamaha and Norton new."

The Yamaha was a collectable bike worth purchasing by itself. It was an A-model TZ 250, meaning that it was a first-year model. It is very light and produces 51 horsepower at 10,000 rpm. The TZ has massive drum brakes because two-stroke engines have virtually no engine braking.

According to Waters, it was the premier privateer racing bike of the mid-1970s. The sale included a second, new old stock disc brake kit, an N.O.S. cylinder barrel, several spare crankshafts, and extra bodywork.

Waters said this bike, a 1973 Norton Monocoque racer, is the most historically significant bike he owns. One of four built, it is the only authentic remaining example. This is the bike in as-found condition. *Jamie Waters*

But then there was the Norton.

"You couldn't really tell much from the photo online, but I could see it had yellow fiberglass bodywork, the Norvil/Lockheed single-disc front brake, and the VIN plate was attached to the spine of the chassis instead of the steering head. Together, these clues suggested it was very likely one of the production factory race bikes, constructed by Norton's race team in Thruxton," he said. "It was almost completely disassembled, but the only part missing was the cylinder head. Judging by the gnarled condition of one of the connecting rods, the head was likely destroyed."

Waters paid $11,000 for the two bikes and all the spare parts. The bikes were located on 32-Mile Road, north of Detroit. When Waters pulled up in the rented box truck, all the parts were spread out in the driveway. By the time he was finished loading, the truck was completely full.

"I was pretty sure the Norton was a factory race version before I saw it in person," he said. "Norton produced 119 of them between 1970 and 1971, and virtually all of them saw race duty from new. These days, genuine examples are rare and desirable, but still a tremendous bargain compared to a Ducati 750 SS or Laverda SFC, bikes which are much more expensive, arguably less capable than a Norton PR, and definitely less rare.

"When I got the bikes home, I sent the Norton's serial number to England, and was right. It was a genuine PR, originally dispatched from Norton's race shop at Thruxton to the U.S. Importer, Berliner, in 1971, then shipped to Blackie's Motorcycles in Detroit."

In the days before lightweight composite materials, this bike was state-of-the-art. The Minnesota brothers purchased the bike for $4,500 when Norton went bankrupt in about 1977, then just stored it in their warehouse until Waters purchased it. The monocoque frame was constructed of 600 pieces of stainless steel and actually included fuel and oil tanks. *Jamie Waters*

DAVE CROXFORD, THE SPONSOR'S DREAM

WHEN it comes to publicity, Dave Croxford is a sponsor's dream. A larger-than-life cockney character, he's constantly hitting the headlines, regardless of his performances on the track.

Remember the TT when he claimed a pig had overtaken him during a practice session! Then there was the BBC documentary *Race of the Powerbikes*. What started out to be a serious look at motor-cycle racing was given a lift, and a lot of humour, by the irrepressible Crockett.

But don't make the mistake of thinking that Dave doesn't take racing seriously. Behind the cheeky exterior, the Ruislip-based racer is dedicated to the sport. After all, he explains: "It's the best job I've ever had."

As he proved at Brands Hatch in October, he can mix it with the best. Then, he won the 750 cc British championship for the John Player Norton team and kept the flag flying in the big-bike races on the Sunday.

Of course, it wasn't Dave's first British title. He took the 350 cc crown back in 1968, riding a 7R AJS. The following year he was top man in the 500 cc class, on a G50 Matchless, and, switching to a Seeley, he won the title again in 1970.

A married man with two children, Dave started racing as a sidecar passenger in 1961. He went solo the next year, but it was not until 1964, when he got a Matchless G50, that he really took up the sport seriously.

When it comes to work, Dave's done just about everything. He's a qualified engineer, but in recent years has dabbled in panel-beating, poodle-clipping and double-glazing.

Crock of all trades? His Aston Martin proves he's made money at it!

When Waters' unique bike was new in 1973, rider Dave Croxford used it to win both the Silverstone round and the overall British 750 cc Championship. *Jamie Waters*

The differences between a standard Norton Commando and a Norton Production Racer are extensive. On the production racing model, beyond the obvious difference in bodywork, the camshaft, pistons, exhaust system, levers and rear-set controls, shouldered aluminum wheels, and cylinder head steady were unique. The PRs, which began as partially completed standard Commandos, were shipped to the race team headquarters at Thruxton, where

In 1974, the same bike was brought to the United States and used by California rider Dave Aldana. Here he poses with the bike prior to the Daytona 200 races that year, where he finished mid-pack. *Dave Aldana*

167

In the heat of battle, Aldana brings the Norton down close to the pegs at Daytona. After this race, the bike went into hibernation for the next three decades. *Dave Aldana*

they were made into racers. Their engines were disassembled, blueprinted, and rebuilt with performance parts by Norton's race team mechanics.

The cylinder heads were ported with bigger valves and a unique intake track while the carburetors utilized racing bellmouths instead of filters. The front brake was a race-only 11.5-inch disc squeezed by a Lockheed Racing caliper mounted to a PR-specific fork leg. The brake rotor bolted to a Campagnolo hub/axle combination. The rear brake drum was modified with cooling ducts.

The final test of every PR was a shakedown session by the team's development rider, Norman White, at the adjacent Thruxton circuit. "Blackie's sold it to Miller, who raced it into the 1980s, when it just became an old, and apparently broken, race bike."

Similar to when Waters purchased the 1931 Harley and the 1947 Indian—planning to sell the Indian and restore the Harley—he had planned to sell the Yamaha and keep the Norton. Until he began to inspect the Yamaha.

"After rebuilding the Norton and racing it, I went through the Yamaha, which needed a lot less than the Norton. I got the TZ running and decided to race it, just to see for myself what a GP-derived racing two-stroke was like.

"It was fantastic.

"Really, both bikes are spectacular," he said. "They are very rare, but also great fun to race. I ended up keeping both of them."

Waters discovered this rare Yamaha TZ250 racer on eBay. The auction included not only a stash of spares, but also a racing Norton. The collection was part of the estate of an owner who cared much for his two bikes. This was the condition of the bike as-found. *Jamie Waters*

With replacement fairings to preserve the originals, Waters has raced the TZ250, a bike he refers to as the ultimate over-the-counter racer, in a vintage race at Summit Point, West Virginia. *Jamie Waters*

MOTORPOLOIST SURVIVOR
by Brad Bowling

Mark Supley, of Scotia, New York, enjoys showing the 1926 Harley-Davidson Model B he spent five years restoring, but the motorcycle racing historian is especially proud of the role his bike played in one of America's earliest forms of mechanized extreme sports.

When Supley is not assembling steam turbines for General Electric at his day job or restoring antique wood boats, he is giving talks at the Saratoga Automobile Museum in Saratoga Springs, New York, on the topic of vintage motorcycle competition.

Supley grew up near two bike dealerships—one selling Kawasakis, the other Hondas—and he credits the exposure for his lifelong obsession with two-wheelers. "The owner of the Honda dealership, Howard Newell, was kind of a gruff character. He didn't want a kid hanging around the shop, but I loved motorcycles.

"I started riding motorcycles when I was 16 years old," he said. "I trail rode, then got into motorcycle scramble racing—what we call motocross today. Howard started sponsoring me, which was funny because when I was a kid he would shoo me away from his junk parts piles."

Mark Supley's 1926 Harley Model B is often mistaken for a former military bike due to its drab olive-green color. The majority of Harley-Davidson motorcycles built between World War I and the Great Depression left the Milwaukee factory with this paint scheme.

Supley got a job in Newell's parts department and built custom bikes on the side. This was during the boom of the 1970s, when his 1942 Harley three-wheeler and pair of Volkswagen-powered trikes were well known with the area's custom chopper crowd.

One day in 1981, Newell came to where Supley was working in the shop and asked a very strange question. "He asked if I had ever seen his old Harley," Supley said.

"I knew he had had one much earlier in his life, but I had no idea he owned anything other than Honda products. He said, 'Come on, it's upstairs.'

"Now, I had been hanging around and working in the dealership most of my life, so I was surprised to hear there was a bike I had not seen before."

Under a tarp in the far corner of the upstairs storage room sat something that barely resembled a motorcycle anymore. The 1926 Model B single-cylinder bike looked as if each of its 55 years of life had been rough ones. The frame was broken, the fork was bent. Newell told him the motor had died tragically when the wrist pin came out and ground a deep groove into the cylinder wall. The transmission was destroyed and the gas tank was damaged. The headlight, floorboard, generator, coil, and dozens of other parts were missing. It was a mess.

When new, the Model B was built for export to the nearly 70 countries in which Harley-Davidson had more than 2,000 dealers. The year 1926 marked the first time since 1918 that Harley installed a single-cylinder engine design in its bikes. Displacing 350 cubic centimeters (21 cubic inches), the B's side-valve powerplant produced 3.5 horsepower. Harley's three-speed transmission in those days had no synchronizer gears, which made shifting a precision task. The total loss oil system meant the driver had to monitor the engine's lubrication and manipulate the pump whenever the single was under load while climbing or accelerating. After being sprayed on the primary chain, the oil was unceremoniously dumped on the ground.

"The Model B was underpowered for its weight," Supley said. "Harley advertised it as getting 80 miles per gallon, but top speed was barely 50 miles per hour. It had external contracting band brakes on the rear and none up front, so stopping is not its strong suit."

Like the majority of Harley-Davidson motorcycles produced between World War I and the start of the Great Depression, Newell's Model B had started life as olive green. Pinstriping was gold and burgundy, but there was little evidence of its former beauty as it decayed above the Honda parts department.

"It had been a generator model, so it originally came with a headlight. Harley was moving away from those boxy gas tanks and had introduced its classic teardrop tank in 1925. Someone had installed a front-wheel brake to Howard's bike at some point, although those were not available on Harleys until 1928. It also had a mud guard at the bottom of the front fender—that was optional in 1926."

Imagining this piece of junk as a shiny new machine took a lot of effort on Supley's part, but he saw the potential. Supley was also drawn to the bike's rather unusual history.

"It had been Howard's first motorcycle," Supley said. "He owned it, traded it, owned it, and traded it again over the years before it was installed in the corner of his dealership."

Howard was a longtime member of the Electric City Riders (ECR), a group of bike enthusiasts that was known as the Schenectady Motorcycle Club until 1942 when they chartered with the American Motorcyclist Association. ECR is still very active in promoting motorcycle competition, but back when Howard was with them the club put on a lot of motorcycle polo matches. "He said his Model B was used as a goalie bike."

Shortly after showing the Harley to Supley, Newell asked him to stop by his office. Thinking the bike was for sale, Supley took his checkbook, but Newell told him he could have the remains of the motorcycle for free if he promised not to sell it or part it out.

Supley agreed to these generous terms and started gathering materials for the project.

"Finding parts for a Model B was extremely difficult," he said. "You can buy what you need for the V-twins of those years, but there was very little available for the singles. This was back in the days before the Internet, so I had to write a lot of letters and make a lot of phone calls to get what I needed, and the process seemed to drag out."

His shopping list for the engine alone included such rare items as a new cylinder, piston rings, and exhaust system. What couldn't be purchased had to be salvaged. Supley recalls that he put 130 hours just into fixing the rear fender.

During the five-year restoration, Supley befriended Louis Lichva, a pillar of the vintage bike community and a founding member of the Antique Motorcycle Club of America (AMCA). Lichva was a local legend whose collection included a 1928 Henderson, a 1940 Indian, and a vintage Ace motorcycle. Lichva acted as an ambassador to the world of motorcycles, giving sidecar rides to the general public at bike shows and fairs. He had been riding vintage motorcycles all his life and shared his wealth of experience with a younger audience.

"Louis knew I was struggling to find the exact right parts for my Model B project," Supley said. "He gave me a wonderful piece of advice that helped me finish and enjoy riding the bike. He said: 'Purists be damned. You've got enough of a motorcycle there—put it together and you'll have fun with it!'"

Lichva passed away before the Harley was finished, but his influence over the project would be felt once again at its show debut.

"When I found out the AMCA national show was coming to nearby Duanesburg," Supley said, "that gave me the final push I needed to finish the restoration.

"I worked eight hours a day for three months to put it together. At Duanesburg, it won the best restored antique honors, and Louis' wife presented me with the award. On the award is a picture of Louis on his motorcycle with a sidecar."

Since restoring the Model B, Supley has loaned it for display to banks, bars, and museums. In an unusual twist of events, Howard Newell asked to borrow the Harley-Davidson—his first motorcycle, and a part of eastern New York's rich two-wheeler history—so he could showcase it in the window of his Honda dealership.

"Motorcycle polo" was a bit of a misnomer from the start, as there was no mallet and the mounted riders scored goals by kicking a standard soccer ball with their feet. The name probably stuck because it sounded more regal—polo was, after all, the "sport of kings," and practically nobody in the United States had heard of soccer in the early 20th century.

Participants were referred to in the press by a variety of names such as "motorpoloists" or "polo cyclists." The birth date and place of this unusual sport

This undated photo from Mark Supley's collection shows two unnamed riders enjoying some motorcycle polo in a dirt field.

This blurry image is all that exists of Supley's polo bike before he restored it. Harley's new style of teardrop tank is easy to spot, however.

are not known, but a *Camden Courier-Post* newspaper clipping from October 29, 1928, documents the results of a well-organized match between rivals representing clubs in Camden and Philadelphia. (Spoiler alert: it was a tie!)

An article in the July 1933 issue of *Popular Science Monthly* by Walter E. Burton indicates there were league and championship games sanctioned by the "American Motor-Cycle Association" in many sections of the country. Five-man teams on stock motorcycles rode around on polo fields, fairgrounds, and football fields measuring approximately 200 by 300 feet. Goalies protected their positions between 14-foot-high posts placed 20 feet apart that were restricted to no more than four inches in diameter. Goalkeepers were allowed to use head, hands, feet, body, or bike to manipulate the ball. Referees were on foot, which required a lot of effort to cover the sometimes dangerous action on the field.

Motorcycle polo games were often part of afternoon-long racing competitions and exhibitions, although some were held as standalone events. Spectacular though it was to watch, motorpolo faded from the American scene in the 1950s. It continues to draw riders and crowds today in many parts of the world and is known as "motoball" in Europe.

FOUR LITTLE INDIANS PULLED FROM A SHED

When Jim Stiner approached a shed in New Jersey, the contents of which he was considering purchasing, there should have been a big sign reading, "Warning: Some Assembly Required!"

What he saw was the mechanical equivalent of a gruesome murder scene. Thousands of parts were scattered everywhere: frames, heads, camshafts, and gears—lots of gears. Amateur gear-heads would have run screaming from the scene, but Stiner kept his cool because somewhere in that awful mess was the realization of a dream.

"This whole obsession with Indians began when I was little, delivering newspapers on my bicycle around the age of 12," Stiner said. "This lady on my route asked if I mowed yards, so I decided to pick up some extra money helping her out. Her son, Anthony Cavazza, was about six years older than me, and he had an Indian, which he kept in the basement near the lawn mower. Every time I went to get the mower, I would spend some time looking at and sitting on that Indian."

Another neighborhood boy named Tom Phillips lived across the street from the Cavazzas, and he had an Indian as well. With so much exposure to the

This is the 1936 Chief that re-ignited Jim Stiner's passion for Indian motorcycles. When he first saw it in 2004, its parts were strewn about a shed in New Jersey like body parts at a crime scene.

175

On the left is the '36 Indian Chief Jim Stiner built for himself. On the right is the '46 Chief he built for a friend.

Springfield, Massachusetts–built two-wheelers, Stiner was smitten. Fortunately, there was somebody closer to home who shared his enthusiasm for riding.

"My older brother always rode motorcycles," Stiner said. "The first bike he brought home was an Indian Scout. It was titled as a '36 but was probably newer than that. It had been a flat-track racer owned by a team mechanic in the 1940s and later belonged to Indian dealer Chuck Myles, who sold it to my brother."

A few years later, Stiner bought his own Indian, also a retired race bike. His brother, who had by then become more interested in Harley-Davidson products, gave him his old Scout and told him to put lights on it so it could be registered for the road.

After getting his driver's license, Stiner rode the Scout during the late 1970s and early 1980s until he bought a Harley Sportster and put the Indian in storage. Stiner began dreaming of the day when he had the resources to own a particular kind of vintage motorcycle.

"I always wanted an Indian Chief," he said, "a 1940-or-later model because they came with the big skirted fenders that look so great. Anthony Cavazza and I were still good friends, and he was still into Indians, so in 2004 I asked him if he knew where I could pick up a Chief that needed to be restored. Anthony was still doing business with Tom Phillips, who had a big collection of Indian parts. He said I should talk to Tom."

Stiner called Phillips, and a couple of months later, he visited the bike collector and took home one of his Indians.

The very next day, Phillips called and asked if Stiner might be interested in buying a lot of his other Indian parts, including several frames and powertrains. All of Stiner's available money had gone toward the first purchase, so he asked his wife how much benefit they were really getting out of the family's savings account.

Stiner's wife did not share his enthusiasm for old motorcycles and failed to see the return on a garage full of two-wheeled basket cases. But Stiner convinced her he could sell some of the inventory quickly and put the cash back into the bank, and maybe even build up the account a bit. She reluctantly agreed, and Stiner drove his cube van to Phillips' house to make the transfer.

"I knew he'd had this stuff for 25 or 30 years," Stiner said, "but I hoped he was keeping it in some kind of good condition. The floor of the shed was literally covered in small parts like gears and nuts and bolts. A lot of the gears were pitted pretty badly. There were parts for eight engines, eight transmissions, eight gear sets, and eight pairs of cylinders on the shelf, but Tom had taken everything apart and strewn stuff all over the place. A lot of guys do that; they disassemble everything on a bike, down to the tiniest springs in a carburetor, and don't even bother identifying or storing things properly."

Jim Stiner was motivated to turn a basket case into this beautiful '46 Chief because he loved the full-fendered Indian look.

Jim Stiner (first from left) sits on the '36 Chief he rebuilt. Vincent Montagna (fourth from left) prepares to enjoy the '46 Chief Stiner and friends built for him. Stiner's childhood friend Anthony Cavazza (second from left) displays his '53 Chief while Cavazza's son Pepper shows off his '40 Scout.

Stiner piled every piece of workable scrap into his truck's 12-foot box and moved the load to its new home. Six months later, Phillips sold Stiner the last remaining bits of his collection, which included yet another nearly complete (though disassembled) bike. "I got some original parts out of that final trip like a speedometer, horn, and a like-new pair of saddlebags. They are the fancy black ones with the white plastic fringe—not my favorite look, but I was glad to have them."

Overall, the separate purchases resulted in a total of four complete motorcycles, all of which have been restored or are nearing completion. From that single shed, Stiner pulled four different Indians: a 1908, 1936, 1941, and 1946.

"The original bike Tom sold me was a 1936 Chief with the 1200cc V-twin engine," Stiner said. "It did not have the big fenders I wanted; however, I fell in love with it because you seldom see these earlier models. It was mostly complete, but the engine was a mismatch. I negotiated a deal and took it home, not realizing at the time I would be going back right away to buy more. I spent all of 2004 finding the missing parts, and finished that bike in 2005. It took me a year to complete, and I've been riding it to events ever since.

"I did not buy the 1908 bike from Tom, but he told me I could sell it for him and send him the money." Turns out, it didn't take long.

"Ken Kelly [featured in *The Vincent in the Barn* as 'Crapoholic,' along with his brother Al] came by to look at the '08 and went nuts for it. He saw it at nine o'clock the night I unloaded the frame from my truck and said he wanted to take it home right then. It was still in pieces, but I put an engine together for him—just tightening everything with my fingers to make sure the parts all fit—and he was back at 10:30 to pay for it.

"I told him that nobody else knew about it yet, but he said, 'I've got to have it now. I don't want it to slip away. Every time I see an Indian from this period, it disappears in no time.' He was probably right to grab it up so fast."

The '46 Chief came by way of a friend from New Jersey. "My friend Vince Montagna had always wanted to own an Indian, and he got real sick a few years ago. I wanted to do something nice for him. I figured I had enough parts to build the '46, so I went to Anthony Cavazza and asked if we could build the 1200cc motor for it. Anthony built the engine for my '36, so I knew it would be a good one. I bought the parts, and Anthony, his son, and I did the work."

The '41 Chief is still a work in progress. "I'm finishing it right now," Stiner said. "The engine is done. The wheels have been restored. The frame, tanks, and fenders have been painted. All I have left is the wiring."

Watching a quartet of Indians go from shed to sharp has been rewarding for Stiner, who believes in riding the old war horses. He and his friends recently rode their Indians 16 hours to a motorcycle meet in Ohio, and the bikes easily withstood the longer scenic tour home.

THE CRAPOHOLICS ARE AT IT AGAIN!

Brothers Al and Ken Kelly are hopeless. If you read *The Vincent in the Barn*, you might remember some of the terrific Indian and Harley barn-finds they had discovered, mostly in their home state of New Jersey.

Well, they never stop searching. To the brothers Kelly, searching for a forgotten bike is always more enjoyable than actual ownership. In fact, they have coined a name for themselves: Crapoholics!

"We're bad," said Ken. "When we go for a ride in the country, we practically stop at every barn and every garage we see. We just knock on doors if we think there might be a motorcycle around somewhere. Some people we meet are friendly and some don't trust you. But we keep trying. You can't worry about rejection. You only have to worry about being shot or being attacked by a dog. Sometimes we don't have to go knocking. Sometimes we'll be on our bikes

As kids, Harley and Indian collectors Al and Ken Kelly each owned Yamaha 100 motorcycles as their first set of wheels. When Al (pictured) found this one for $300 40 years later, he had to buy it. The bike will become his son's first as well. *Ken Kelly*

and someone will come up to us and say, 'My dad had one of those.' Our next question is, 'Is it still around? Do you have any parts or photos?'"

So sit back and enjoy a few more bike-in-the-barn stories by the original Crapoholics: Al and Ken Kelly.

Childhood Yamaha

Al and Ken Kelly work together, so it's not unusual for them to take a coffee break and find motorcycles while they are driving to the local deli: Once, in the deli parking lot, they saw a van with signs painted on the sides advertising that the driver handled estate sales and clean-ups.

"I'm not afraid to talk to strangers, so I walked up to the man and asked if he ever found old motorcycles," said Al. The man said no, but that he's always on the lookout. So Al said thank you and gave the man his business card. "If you ever come across something interesting and you're looking to get rid of it, give me a call."

The 40-year-old bike accumulated less than 1,300 miles before going into storage. Ordering $25 worth of parts and investing a few hours' labor was all it took to get the bike running like new again. *Tom Cotter*

Al and Ken went back to work and didn't think much about the chance encounter. But then, the very next day, Al received a phone call from the man.

"Son," the man said. "I forgot all about the bike in my garage. When I was a kid during the gas crunch, my father went out and bought a little Yamaha 100 to drive to work. He never used it much, and I still have it."

Al went to the man's house to see the bike. It was buried in the garage and all but forgotten under a tarp. The barn-find Yamaha was like a trip back in time for the brothers. Decades earlier, he and Ken both owned similar bikes. "My brother had a green 1972 Yamaha 100 when we were kids," said Al. "And I had a 1973. This was exactly the same bike. I thought it would be fun to buy this Yamaha and ride it to my brother's shop to surprise him."

The man told Al that he and his brothers were all six-foot-plus, so none of them were ever able to fit on the little bike. So years ago, it was parked in the garage and forgotten. "One time we tried to start it, but the seals had gone bad," said the man. "It smoked like a bear because it sucked engine oil from the crankcase and into the combustion chamber."

So it sat for 40 years.

The man wanted $400 for the bike, but Al negotiated, saying that since it needed seals, it wasn't worth that much. They agreed on $300 and Al loaded it into his truck. "New, these sold for about $400," said Al. "I remember I paid $300 for mine in 1974. I was the second owner."

Al unloaded it and kick-started the bike. The man was right; all it needed was a little gas, and it smoked a lot. He went to a local motorcycle shop that specialized in Japanese bikes. The shop owner's first bike as a kid was also a Yamaha 100, so he lit up and told Al exactly what he needed to buy and fix his new discovery.

"It cost me $25 for the parts and $8 shipping," he said. "I fixed the seals and it runs perfectly. The gas tank had been repainted at some point, but within a week a friend found one on eBay in the same green color. We bought it and installed it without even cleaning it. It even had a gas cap."

Other than the tank, the bike is all original, right down to all those little plastic wire clips, the original key, and key fob.

"Even at my age, in my fifties, I have great fun hopping on this bike and riding it around the yard," he says. "It will be my son's first motorcycle," Al said of his three-year-old. "I can teach him how to wrench on it. He was only a year and a half when he went for a ride with me on my Harley. Somehow I think he'll be into bikes at an early age."

With a dad like Al Kelly, and an uncle like Ken, the kid probably doesn't have any other choice.

Seriously Old Indian

When friends saw the meager assortment of parts Ken Kelly was starting with, they all said he would never, ever find the rest of the parts to restore that bike. "I said to them, 'You know, I'm pretty good at routing things out,'" Ken said. "I know a lot of people around the country, and I've been into this hobby for an awfully long time. I had no doubt."

According to Kelly, the most important thing is to find out not only what parts collectors have, but what parts they need for bikes they are restoring. "If you need a rare gas tank, and a collector has one, it's probably not for sale unless you are willing to pay crazy, crazy money," said Ken. "But if you have something that they need to trade, you'll get the tank."

What bike are we discussing?

A 1908 Indian Twin. A rare, rare bike.

Through the vintage-motorcycle grapevine, Ken Kelly heard that a man who collected and dismantled many bikes—filling his garage in the process—moved to Washington State and left all those parts behind.

The man's friend, Jimmy, was selling those parts for the owner.

Ken was looking at the racks of parts when his eyes stopped at a set of engine cases.

Soon after purchasing his '08 Indian Twin project, Ken Kelly began assembling the components on a wooden stand in his shop. The man who sold it told Kelly there was a frame hanging in the shed that looked like it was for a bicycle. *Ken Kelly*

This is how the '08 Indian looks today. Because of the rarity of parts for this vintage bike, it took Kelly 10 years to gather enough parts to assemble it to this condition. The bike was built for static display purposes, so he has not tried to start it. *Ken Kelly*

Kelly traded a bunch of Knucklehead parts for this original-paint gas tank and sourced this early aluminum 1912 New Jersey motorcycle license plate. The plate numerals slide in like "Chiclets" according to Kelly. *Ken Kelly*

One proud Crapoholic—Ken Kelly proudly sits between his "unrestored" 1908 Indian Twin and his "Goodies cabinet." His brother Al also has a collection of similar… crap.
Ken Kelly

"I'm looking through the mountain of parts," Ken said. "I'm looking at about a dozen sets of engine cases for the 1930s and 1940s. All of a sudden, I saw this little, bitty set of cases. My heart jumped, because I recognized them; these cases are very unique, very small, and completely round. I asked Jimmy what they were. He said he thought they were for a 1912. I pulled them down and looked at them. I said to myself, 'My God, it's a twin cylinder.'

"When he saw the look on my face, Jimmy said, 'Those aren't for sale. The guy wants those back.'

"It was just two cases—no crankshaft or pistons—that were wired together. But once I saw them, I wasn't interested in anything else."

Ken tried to be cool, but he clearly wasn't interested in leaving without a deal on those engine cases. Early Indian twins are extremely rare, and only about a dozen exist in the world.

"Look, I'm local," Ken said to Jimmy. "Do me a favor; call the guy and see if he wants to sell the engine because I'm really interested." Jimmy agreed to call the owner, but Ken was in agony as he waited for a phone call.

Ken asked Jimmy if there might be any other parts that might go with those cases. "There is an old frame, which looks like it's for a bicycle, hanging on the wall of the shed," Jimmy said.

"It took me months to finally make the deal," Ken said. "Jimmy kept going back to the guy's barn and finding more parts for me. Eventually he dragged out the main frame section, the crankshaft, pistons, and rods."

Ken spent about $5,000 for these initial parts. He said that with very rare bikes, prices are devalued unless they are nearly complete when purchased. Because parts are so difficult to source, the likelihood of completing the restoration is very low. But once a significant amount of parts are secured, the value of the project doubles. "So I started this restoration with just a frame and a motor; that was it. Nobody thought I'd be able to complete the restoration with just those parts."

It took Ken 10 years to collect all the parts to assemble his project. His only guide was a couple of old photographs. He said there aren't a lot of people who actually know much about this era of bikes. "Ten years is considered warp-speed for putting one of these together," he said.

Ken has also collected some very rare accessories.

"I found this carbide gas taillight," he said. "The light canister was sitting on one flea market table and I picked it up. Then I walked over to the other flea market table and picked up the lamp. They fit together. It was the only taillight I've ever seen like it, and it was like brand new!"

He also found a Veeder Cyclometer, a speedometer/odometer accessory that attaches to the frame and the wheel. He found a rare license plate, the oldest known motorcycle plate in New Jersey. It is from 1912 and made of aluminum, and as Ken describes, the numerals slide in like Chiclets. Many collectors didn't know such a plate existed.

"I needed a gas tank, which I knew was going to be very hard to find," Ken said. "But I met a man at the Davenport swap meet who had a correct 1908 tank. Problem was, he didn't want to sell it."

Kelly had met the worst kind of swap meet vendor—the kind who brings rare parts to a meet, not to sell, but simply to show off. That's when he turned on the salesman's charm. "I chatted him up and found out he was into Knuckleheads, so over the course of the winter, I sent him photos of all the Knucklehead parts I had to trade," he said. "And I told him that I really needed his tank because it had original paint, and I wanted to keep my bike all original."

Eventually, they swapped treasures. Ken got not only a much-needed gas tank, he also secured a correct seat and a set of handlebars.

Luckily, he sourced a tool bag and a complete toolset as well.

"Even mounting the tires was a time-consuming project," he said.

Early Indians have an extremely rare "double-clinching" rim design. It is made only for a tire with a unique bead design. Indian changed their rim design in 1909 or 1910, so finding a double-clinching rim is as rare as it is complicated. "I had to take a standard-beaded tire and cut into it with a razor blade," he said. "It took me about four hours to cut each tire to fit. And if I made a mistake, the tires cost about $300 each. I had to take my time."

The only pieces that Ken is still searching for are the front fender, muffler, and battery tube. But he is having fun showing his Indian. And he has no doubt that he will one day find those pieces as well.

Restoring the Patina

Sounds like an oxymoron, doesn't it? But the Kelly Brothers have methods for restoring motorcycles while making them appear to be fresh from the barn.

"I've done a few things with spray cans that have surprised me," said Ken. "I'll spray primer on frame members instead of gloss paint. And I've chemically rusted items. I had to make a new cover for a tool box, because it was missing. So I rusted the new metal, not to fool someone into thinking it was original, but so that the new part did not jump out while someone is looking at the bike. It would look like a pimple."

When Ken Kelly needs parts with patina, he just goes to the vintage truck junkyard he keeps behind his house for cloth-covered wiring, hoses, clamps, etc. Parts for several of his "original" restorations have been sourced from these trucks. *Ken Kelly*

Ken has wetted a piece of metal, chemically rusted it, and put blotches of paint on it to make it look surprisingly old. He said to rust a piece of metal, he goes to a gunsmith shop. "It's a long process, but I've done it enough to know that it can give good results," he said.

Ken uses other methods for making a replacement item appear to be vintage. "I'll make a piece, and hand file or use emory paper on it," he said. "Then I'll whack it with wooden sticks to make it look forged. I'll get some really gritty, dirty grease from underneath one of my old pickup trucks and smear it over the part. Then I'll take the part and cook it on top of some bricks with propane until it bubbles. When it cools and I wipe it off, it looks pretty old."

Ken said that to rebuild electrical components, he'll go back to his old-truck junkyard in the woods behind his house and use the old cloth wiring from under the truck's dash and engine compartment. He'll also rub that dirty grease on the wires to give them a 100-year-old look instead of just 50 years old.

Once, Ken needed a hub for one of his very early Indian projects. So he purchased a 100-year-old bike just for the parts. "It was already rusty and the hub was so close to the Indian's, that I bought the whole thing," he said. "I used the pedals and took apart the wheels for the spokes and the hubs."

Ken said that cash doesn't always work when you need to buy a part from a collector. So he'll collect all kinds of components and store them in his "goody cabinet," and he'll use them strictly for swapping purposes.

"Some guys are wealthy enough that any amount of cash doesn't do anything for them," he said. "But if you have the right part, they get all excited." In the vintage vehicle business, no amount of money makes up for the part you need. Trading, though, is akin to a secret handshake, a bargain between collectors and restorers that transcends any monetary values.

THE TWO RULES OF MOTORCYCLE BARN-FINDING

There are two basic rules to discovering long hidden bikes. Rule Number One: Talk about old motorcycles to everyone you meet.

Just ask Chris Slawski of Medford Lakes, New Jersey. He has the enviable job of being a service trainer for Subaru of America, which is based in Cherry Hill, New Jersey. "I talk to service managers and mechanics all day," Slawski said. "These guys have been around the block and usually have cars or bikes as hobbies." Slawski's territory is the entire United States, including Alaska and Hawaii.

"You never really know the person on the other end of the phone line, but little by little, you find out about their lives."

In addition to his telephone work, Slawski spends about eight weeks a year traveling around the country giving seminars on warrantee claims. That's when he can finally meet some of the folks he has been talking with on the phone. During the seminars, he's all business, but during lunch breaks, he meets with his students one-on-one. "When you meet them in person, their stories start coming out," he said. "You find out what they do on their off-time."

The 1970 T100 C had been ridden hard and put away wet, but Slawski knew he could restore the bike for less than the $500 the new owner was selling it for. *Chris Slawski*

From the moment he sold his own Triumph T 100 to a co-worker, Chris Slawski regretted his decision. So when he heard about a near replacement for $500, he jumped on it. *Chris Slawski*

During those lunch breaks, Slawski is quick to bring up his love for old motorcycles, particularly Triumphs.

Even though he has been a trainer for Subaru for six years, prior to that he worked as a service writer and mechanic in a Harley-Davidson dealership in Burlington, New Jersey, about 20 miles east of Philadelphia near Atlantic City.

"I had owned several Harleys, but I was looking to pick up a project bike," he said. "One of the guys at the dealership said that a friend of his was selling a '79 Triumph Bonneville, so I picked that up and did a frame-up restoration." Thus began his passion for Triumph brand motorcycles.

He sold the '79 Bonneville and picked up a '70 T 100 C from a man in Massachusetts. He brought the bike home, but it sat and sat in his garage.

"It sat for a few years, and I really hadn't made much progress on it, so I sold it to one of my co-workers at the Harley dealership. I made a couple of hundred dollars on it and sold it for $1,400."

He immediately regretted his decision.

Meanwhile, the new owner, Tim, invested a little bit of work in restoring the cylinder head and tuning the carbs. "He got it running smoother, and I had the itch to buy it back," Slawski said. "He said he would sell it to me for $5,000. I thought about it and thought about it. I really wanted it back, but he didn't own it that long, and hadn't done that much work to it to justify $5,000."

The bike had been stored in a heated garage since being taken off the road in 1977. Slawski plans to do all the restoration work except for paint. *Chris Slawski*

Not for sissies; the era this Triumph was modified is obvious by the rear sissy bar. But the restoration of a bike in this condition is not for sissies either!

Included in the Triumph package deal was a second bike, a 1968 T100 R, a hotted up version with dual carbs. The bike is basically complete with the exception of one missing side cover. *Chris Slawski*

That's where Rule Number One of barn-finding comes in: talk about old motorcycles to everyone you meet.

"So I was giving a training class, and during lunch I tell all my students that I'm into old Triumph motorcycles," Slawski said. "So this one guy, who works in a Michigan Subaru dealership but lives near Akron, Ohio, he tells me he has a couple of old Triumphs in his garage. He had no idea what they were, however."

Slawski asked the man for the VINs: one was a 1970 Triumph T 100 C, which was basically the same bike that Slawski had recently sold, and the other was a 1968 T 100 R, a spiced-up version of the T 100 C, with dual carburetors.

He had stored them in his garage for about 20 years and really knew nothing about them. The man also owned, but was not selling, a Triumph 5T Enduro. Slawski's best guess is that the man bought all three bikes in a package deal 20 years earlier and planned to use the other two bikes' parts as scrap for his Enduro.

"I asked how much he wanted for the bikes, and he said $500 each," Slawski said. "So the good news was that I was able to replace the T 100 C that I sold for the same amount of money as Tim wanted to sell it to me for, minus one zero," he added with a smile.

Slawski plans to sell the '68 T 100 R and restore the T 100 C. "I'll do all the restoration on it myself except for paint," he said.

If this bike could talk, what would it tell us of only commuting 7,571 miles in the past four decades? Slawski's desire is to sell the T100 R; the lucky person who buys it will have a terrific starting point for a restoration. *Chris Slawski*

He still hasn't made the trip from New Jersey to Akron, Ohio, to pick up his two barn-find Triumphs. He said he'll probably make the 20-hour round trip in the spring.

"From the photos, the bikes look to be 90 percent complete," he said. "The 1970 has low exhaust pipes, which are not correct, and the '68 is missing a side cover. But these are not hard items to get; I'll get most of them from a couple of guys who work at the old Harley dealership where I used to work. They used to be Triumph mechanics and still have boatloads of parts."

When he's done with the restoration, what will he do with the bike?

"I won a 2007 Harley Superglide Custom that I ride a lot," he said. "Besides, I'm six feet three inches tall and weigh 300 pounds. If I rode that Triumph 500, I'd look like a bear on a tricycle.

"The restoration will keep me out of trouble. When it's done, I'll just keep it as artwork. Besides, it seems that when I sell something, I just start looking to replace the same bike I just sold. So as long as I have garage space, I won't sell it."

Just to make it clear, Rule Number One doesn't just work with motorcycles. Slawski also owns a '69 Camaro and a '64 Pontiac GTO, both barn-finds and both discovered by talking to everyone he meets.

Oh, and you're probably wondering about Rule Number Two?

Just repeat Rule Number One.

CHAPTER FIVE

Rare Finds and One-of-a-Kinds

GODDESS OF THE HUNT

With his discovery of a nearly complete 1965 Ducati Mark 3 in the attic of a Texas motorcycle shop while on a parts hunt in 1991, Rich Mooradian added an iconic production racer to his growing collection of Italian sportbikes.

On the timeline of motorcycles manufactured in the 20th century, the Ducati brand is a relatively new one. Unlike most of the legendary two-wheeler makes discussed in this book—names such as Harley-Davidson, Indian, and Vincent—Ducati motorcycles are entirely a post–World War II phenomenon, just one arm of a family-run empire with wide-ranging interests.

Antonio Cavalieri Ducati and his three sons started the Società Radio Brevetti Ducati in 1926 in Bologna, Italy, to make radio components, but it was clear the family had big plans for expansion. By the 1930s, the Ducati name was known around the world for its radios, and the company had offices in New York, London, Paris, Sydney, and Caracas.

In 1935, Ducati began construction on what would become a sprawling, 3,500-employee factory/technology center in Bologna's Borgo Panigale. German troops took over the factory in 1943 for munitions manufacture, and

Rich Mooradian has an unusual connection to his bike's history. His father was a navigator on a B-24 Liberator bomber and saved some of the sortie documents. The paperwork shows Bologna, the Ducati factory's location in Italy, as one of the raids scheduled for 1944. The racing seat with cover is not factory-correct for this 1965 Ducati Diana, but it is a popular original accessory that was available in the mid-1960s.

Since the owner/restorer of this Diana enjoys riding it on occasion—as can be observed by the "bluing" of the exhaust tube chrome—he has installed a replica megaphone muffler with baffles to reduce the engine noise. He has, however, an original megaphone (nothing more than a pretty, chrome straight pipe).

Allied bombing, under the codename Operation Pancake, nearly destroyed it on October 12, 1944, with the combined might of 75 B-24 Liberators.

Despite a blow that would have permanently ended most industrial aspirations, the Ducati brothers entered the post-war market with renewed enthusiasm and products as diverse as miniature cameras and an auxiliary engine for bicycles called the Cucciolo.

Clip-on engines for bicycles were nothing new in the industry; their use predated purpose-built motorcycles. It was Ducati's marketing strength and production techniques that made the SIATA-designed, 48cc four-stroke, overhead-valve single with unusual pullrods a success throughout Europe.

The 17-pound Cucciolo, or "little pup," became a complete turnkey moped in 1950 capable of 40 miles per hour and a claimed 180 miles per gallon of precious gasoline, giving Ducati entrée into the fast-growing motorcycle market.

In 1953, the Ducati organization was divided into two production channels—one for electronics, the other, named Ducati Meccanica, for motorcycles and marine powerplants. The new heads of the motorcycle

Rich Mooradian stripped his attic-found Diana to the frame for a full restoration.

division wanted the Ducati brand to dominate its market, but that was unlikely to happen with its line of pleasant, efficient scooters and mopeds.

Motorsports competition was the only way to rise above the other post-war offerings, which is why the company hired a brilliant young mechanical engineer, Fabio Taglioni, in 1954 to develop a new series of sportbikes.

Taglioni was working in the racing department of Italian rival motorcycle maker Mondial when Ducati Meccanica's general manager asked him to build 100 bikes for the nine-day Tour of Italy competition. The 98cc 100 Gran Sport Marianna he developed during the next six months became the company's first race-ready model, and the upstart team handily won the Tour at an average speed of 61.5 miles per hour.

The basic architecture of that first engine, with its bevel-drive valvetrain and overhead camshaft, would evolve and grow in displacement for the next two decades and cement Ducati's reputation as a maker of world-class racing motorcycles.

In 1961, pressure from American and British importers to address the popular 250cc-class in their respective markets persuaded Ducati to introduce the single-cylinder Monza and a Diana model equipped for racing. Three years later, when Ducati fitted all its 250cc bikes with new five-speed transmissions, the top model was the competition-bred Mach 1, which featured 10.0:1 compression, a high-lift camshaft, and bigger valves.

Ducatis imported to the States in the 1960s were often fitted with more "American" handlebars before they were sold. Restorers have found many of the low-set clip-ons tucked way back on dealership shelves.

Much of the Mach 1's desirable performance components carried over to the 1965 250 Mark 3 Diana, a dusty example of which that caught Rich Mooradian's eye while he was searching for Ducati parts in a shop near Dallas/Ft. Worth.

"When I graduated from college," Mooradian said, "I really wanted a Ducati. I was lucky enough to find a 1979 Dharma SS, one of the bevel-drive V-twins, and I fell in love with the company's motorcycles. Their aluminum engines are precision instruments, like Swiss watches. Ducatis are always leagues ahead of other machines from the same era."

He was living in the Minneapolis/St. Paul area and enjoying the active foreign motorcycle community there when he heard about a shop that specialized in Ducatis, Nortons, and BMWs in Texas.

"I was restoring my first Ducati at the time—this was around 1991. It was a '69 350cc single Desmodromic, and I needed some parts I couldn't find in Minnesota. That Desmo engine was new in 1968, and it was extremely rare to see any of the early models. I decided to visit Storm's Cycles in Texas during a trip for a business seminar."

Storm's is housed in a large brick building on Jefferson Street in Grand Prairie, and its 90-year-old owner, Doc, is an institution among foreign bike enthusiasts. He is also, by all accounts, the definition of a gracious southern gentleman.

"A guy from my seminar gave me a ride to Doc's in his rental car," Mooradian said. "He wasn't into motorcycles; he just thought it was interesting that I had to travel the country looking for parts to restore my old motorcycle.

"Doc told me that what I wanted was in the attic and that I could help myself. He didn't know how accurate his words were that 'what I wanted' was up there."

The attic was a large room with old parts organized by brand and function. There were motorcycles, frames, and complete engines scattered about. There was no ramp available to move big components up and down; Doc used an old-fashioned hoist for that chore. Mooradian could not believe he was standing in such a treasure trove of Ducati and Norton parts. "If I had had my wits about me," he said, "I would have made an offer on the whole attic. That stuff would be worth a fortune now. I was distracted, though, by the sight of a Mark 3 Diana leaning against the wall, all covered in dust. There were a few pieces missing, so I didn't realize at first I was looking at one of the most desirable Ducati models of the 1960s."

Knowing that Ducati only sold approximately 1,000 of the production racers worldwide, Mooradian verified that it had the special Mark 3 engine identification and took inventory of what was missing.

Dianas were different from other 250s in that they were equipped with a competition kit that included a megaphone exhaust, Veglia Borletti tachometer, rear-set foot pegs, clip-on handlebars with a smooth top clamp, and a special curved kick start lever to clear the pegs. Because American riders had not yet adapted to the café racer riding position, importers generally sold the high-strung Dianas with touring handlebars and standard foot pegs and put the "good stuff" on the shelf.

Doc Storm's Diana was wearing a 20-year-old license plate and had not run in a while.

"It was mostly complete," Mooradian said, "and I wanted to buy it. But Doc thought his son might want the bike, so I left Texas without it. A few weeks later, after investigating more of the history of the Mark 3, I called Doc and he sold it to me. It wasn't like I was dealing with an old widow. Since he was an expert and knew what he had, I paid the going rate for it. He shipped it to me in Minnesota."

During his restoration, Mooradian spent a lot of time tracking down the missing Euro-spec race kit parts, an original megaphone exhaust, and a fairing-like number plate. He likes to ride the Diana, so Mooradian installed a replica exhaust equipped with noise baffling; otherwise, the high-compression single is too loud with the factory-spec straight pipe.

"As it came from Ducati, the Mark 3 was a café racer with a headlight and taillight," he said. "It has a bell-mouth intake for air without a filter. You can't drive it on anything other than a clean road or the carburetor will suck in the dust.

"It's hard to believe these bikes are so fast for only 250cc. They only weighed 250 pounds, and that lightness was part of Ducati's philosophy. A motorcycle magazine in 1964 clocked a Mark 3 at 110 miles per hour."

Since completion, the racing Ducati, named for the Roman goddess of the hunt, has joined Mooradian's Ducati 750 and a Moto Morini in his collection, which is shaping up to be a tribute to beautiful, superfast Italian motorcycles.

20TH CENTURY CYCLE

Imagine what most collectors would say if they saw Carl Haren drag racing his 100-year-old motorcycle!

Well, Haren doesn't care what they would say. He's been having fun with this 1912 Pierce since he was a kid, and he's not about to stop now.

Search "1912 Pierce Mooneyes Drags" on YouTube to see Haren pedaling his vintage motorcycle to give it a bit more "boost" at an Irwindale drag strip. The result? A somewhat less-than-blistering 27.97 mph set in the eighth mile.

The bike, which celebrated its 100th birthday in 2012, was built in Buffalo, New York, a spin-off of the company that built Pierce-Arrow automobiles. Pierce traced its roots in manufactured goods back to 1865, and added bicycles to its offerings in the late 1890s. Motorcycles followed with the first model on sale in 1909. Ultimately, 320 were manufactured with four-cylinder engines, 80 with one-cylinder engines, and 32 with high-compression one-cylinder engines. Pierce Cycle Company went bankrupt in 1914.

Haren, who is known among his friends as Carburetor Carl, owns one of the high-compression bikes, a top-of-the-line model that was often used for racing.

This is a modern interpretation of a scene Carl Haren remembers from childhood. Haren and his brothers used to play on this motorcycle when they visited their uncle in Galesburg, Illinois, during the summer. It never ran, but they had fun rolling it down hills. *Carl Haren*

The Pierce motorcycle was manufactured by the Pierce Arrow automobile company of Buffalo, NY. This is the rather ornate badge on the steering head. *Carl Haren*

The Pierce was disabled for many years because of a missing magneto (pictured). Since taking possession of the bike as an adult, he has located not one, but two magnetos. *Carl Haren*

202

These days, Haren still has fun with the Pierce. The 100-year-old bike is regularly shown at Concours events and even occasionally drag races! *Carl Haren*

His bike was sold new in Buffalo, New York, to a World War I veteran who didn't ride it much. The veteran owned the bike until about 1922 and stored it in a shed. Haren's uncle, Gus Lambert, was an enterprising young fellow. He and his brother, both in their mid-teens, owned a 1917 Harley-Davidson. In 1922, when Gus spotted the seldom-used Pierce, he offered the owner a trade. "Give me the Pierce and $10 and you can have the Harley."

"My uncle knew that the Pierce was a much better motorcycle than the Harley," said Haren. "The veteran who owned the Pierce thought he was stepping up to a Harley, but he was actually stepping down."

Haren's uncle and his brother rode the Pierce back and forth from their home in Galesburg, Illinois, to school from 1922 to 1925. At that time, in rural Illinois, driver's licenses were not necessary.

Life seemed good to the Pierce-riding brothers until the magneto broke. The boys sent the busted magneto to an electrical shop in Peoria, Illinois, for repair. When they returned to the shop a couple weeks later, the business was gone along with their magneto.

The brothers lugged their broken Pierce into another shed and forgot about it.

In 1956, Gus Lambert's four nephews came to stay with him on the farm for the summer. The youngest of those brothers, Carl, was 8 years old. "One of the treats of going to the farm for the summer was being able to drag his old motorcycle out of the shed and play with it," recalled Carl Haren, now 61. "Some pieces had been removed from the Pierce—a pedal here, a carburetor there—and used around the farm, but we were able to use a stick for a pedal and pedal the motorcycle around the barn yard."

An early speed-seeking thrill for Haren and his brothers was to push the Pierce up the hill on the property and coast down into the yard. "My uncle kept geese on the property, and these geese would torment us kids," he said. "They would pinch us with their beaks and chase us around the yard. But when we came down that hill, honking a horn that sounded like a goose being grabbed, we were able to chase the geese. It was payback, to get even with those stupid birds."

Gus got a kick watching his nephews on his old bike. They were determined to have fun on that motorcycle even though it didn't run, and had decrepit, leaky tires. "We would pump up the tires and the tubes would hold air for about 15 minutes," Haren said. "So we'd use the hand pump and get about four laps up and down the hill before the tires went flat again. We'd spend all day on that motorcycle."

One day in the 1970s, Haren got a call from his uncle.

"You guys have to come back up here and pick this thing up because I'm tearing down the shed and have no place to store it," said Uncle Gus.

By this time, Haren was a full-fledged motorcyclist, a collector of mostly old Honda and Yamaha race bikes. His goal was to refurbish the old Pierce, but not restore.

But driving from California to Illinois to pick up an old motorcycle would have been difficult. Luckily, Haren knew a motorcycle racer, Scotty Parker, who would be racing just 12 miles from Uncle Gus' house in Galesburg. "Scotty picked up the motorcycle for me, stored it in his trailer, and dropped it off in California when the circuit brought him to Nevada and San Jose," explained Haren.

"Even though I never restored it, I've invested about $40,000 in it," Haren said. "The magneto was missing, so it took seven years to locate a replacement. I paid $1,000 for it. Then I found a second one two months later, which I bought as well."

Haren located tires through Coker. They were made in Vietnam in the 1970s and cost $1,200 for the pair.

As he dug into the old bike, Haren discovered that the threads on every nut and bolt had a unique 30-pitch thread angle. "Apparently the reason for the unique threads were so no one else could use Pierce parts on their bikes, and Pierce parts had to be used on their bikes," Haren explained. "They probably made all their own hardware."

The front four or five inches of the frame had rotted badly. Haren found a welder who was able to sleeve the missing frame tubes. It's nearly impossible to detect the repair.

"The bike still has the original paint, original rust, and original grease," he said. "When I take it to a concours, they always take points away because of the grease. They ask me to remove it. But I'm not going to clean it off because the grease is 100 years old. I'm winning those shows. I've won five out of seven concours and took two second places."

Because the bike is 100 years old, many top-flight shows are keen to have it displayed, including the famed Pebble Beach Concours d'Elegance. "It ain't no trailer queen, I'll tell you that," he said. "Sometimes I'll fire it up just to hear it run."

FOLLOW THE NUMBERS

This story is not about the BMW R69S Sam Bernstein purchased on eBay a couple of years ago, although that bike does play a supporting role in the larger story.

Like many of us, Bernstein is slightly addicted to following interesting bikes on the Internet. But meeting him at his place of business—the prestigious Fairmont Hotel in San Francisco—you'd never guess he is actually a motorcycle geek. For decades, Bernstein has been the go-to guy for wealthy individuals who desire Oriental art and jade. It's a business he takes seriously, having built a reputation as a knowledgeable and trusted dealer of art.

But to hear him talk after hours about bikes and cars, one quickly realizes this man is equally comfortable in the gear-head world as well.

Sam Bernstein was never truly a gear-head, but his older brother certainly was. Kenny Bernstein, seven years Sam's senior, was consumed by with speed and drag racing as a teen. When faced with a decision to remain in the restaurant business or become a full-time drag racer, Kenny went to his father for advice.

Owner Sam Bernstein and his eBay-find 1966 BMW R69S "bobber" on the day his new purchase arrived. He thought the bike looked cool and successfully bid it up to $6,800 before the auction ended. *Sam Bernstein*

The bike coming together. Here is Bernstein (right) and restorer James De Alba, the BMW restoration expert from Northern California. *Sam Bernstein*

"Can you make any money drag racing?" his father asked. "Not really," Kenny said, "sponsors don't pay much money."

Who watches drag racing?

"Mostly people who drink beer," Kenny said.

Kenny's father, who knew nothing about drag racing, gave his son an answer that changed the business model of drag racing forever.

"If they drink beer, go find a beer sponsor," he told his son. "And don't sell it as racing, sell it as advertising."

What Sam's brother did has become entry-level canon at business schools ever since; Kenny painted his dragster and the huge hauler with Budweiser colors and logos, then he parked it at the Anheuser-Busch headquarters campus in St. Louis before the employees arrived at work. They all noted the Bud-logoed car, and talked about it all day in the office.

At lunchtime, Kenny fired up the dragster's engines, which literally shook the building.

He left St. Louis with a sponsor, and forever changed the auto racing sponsorship business in the process. The relationship he began that day lasted 30 years and resulted in six National Hot Rod Association Championships.

The R69 went through a thorough restoration. Here is the motor case, connecting rod, and crankshaft during disassembly. *Sam Bernstein*

Meanwhile, young Sam was standing on the sidelines, absorbing all the dialogue. It's no wonder he has gasoline running in his veins, even though he makes his living as a fine-art dealer.

Bernstein liked the looks of a certain BMW R69S he had been tracking on eBay. The seller, who had been a BMW Motorcycle Club concours judge, was a respected member who had discovered the R69S languishing on somebody's front porch. It was grungy, so he decided that rather than restore it, he would have a little fun and convert it to a bobber.

For those not familiar with the term, bobbers were made popular in the Marlon Brando, born-to-be-wild days of returning World War II veterans in the late 1940s and 1950s. Bobbers were stripped-down motorcycles that usually had no front fender, a chopped rear fender, and low handlebars.

Bernstein swapped his R69S for a rarer 1957 R69. Here the frame is being readied for paint. Little did he know that his bike, frame #652581, carried a famous pedigree. *Sam Bernstein*

Bernstein saw a bobber on his computer monitor and thought it was cool.

"The bike was in Florida, and I'm in California, so I bought it sight-unseen," he said. "But I thought what he did to it was really striking, so I bid $5,500, and went up in $100 increments to $6,000. Then $6,500. When the bidding was over, I owned it for $6,800."

Bernstein arranged for shipping from Florida to his local BMW dealership. Before he arrived to check out his new acquisition, another customer at the shop, who was there buying parts, inquired about it.

"I know that bike," said the customer to a salesman. "That's the bike I just saw on eBay." The customer left his business card with the salesman and asked if he could have the new owner contact him.

When Bernstein arrived, he discovered that the bike was going to need a lot more work than he originally thought, so he decided to investigate a restorer.

"At that same moment, the salesman told me there was a guy in today, and was familiar with the bike," Bernstein said. "He handed me his card. It read: 'James De Alba, Sonoma Classic Motorbikes.' I figured, All right! A restorer."

Bernstein drove to Sonoma, about one hour north of San Francisco, and met with De Alba. De Alba showed him a BMW R69 on his workbench he had just begun restoring. The frame was bent and rusted, but the engine and frame had matching serial numbers. Then he showed Bernstein the gas tank and fenders, which had already been repainted and pinstriped.

"The paint was spectacular and the pinstriping was outstanding," he said.

De Alba made Bernstein an offer: "The R69 is much rarer than the R69S because far fewer were manufactured," De Alba asserted. He suggested Bernstein swap his R69S bobber for the rusty and bent-frame R69, plus give De Alba some cash, and in return Bernstein would restore the R69 like new for him.

"He said it would be beautiful when it was finished," Bernstein said.

Bernstein liked the rarity of the R69, of which about 2,000 were manufactured as opposed to about 12,000 R69S models manufactured. "I was in love with the paint quality of the gas tank and fenders, so when he suggested that, I agreed," Bernstein said. "We shook hands on it. He was happy and I was happy.

"Seven months later, James called and told me the bike was finished. It was gorgeous. It was everything I expected and more."

Still mounted on his gas tank is the original brass German motorcycle club badge. *Sam Bernstein*

In the meantime, Bernstein began to apply his skills as an art dealer and historian to the documentation of his new motorcycle. "I always research items that I handle," he said. "Like who has owned them, where they have been, what books they may have been published in, and where they have been exhibited. These things add to the provenance of an object and enhance its value.

"Also, it's like a detective story, and I have a very strong sense of curiosity about these things."

This is where the story gets really interesting. The last registered owner Bernstein could discover was a doctor in the Oakland area, who titled it in 1985. Bernstein investigated

The finished product. Bernstein took possession of his newly restored R69. His bike had been delivered new to German motorcycle road racing ace Georg Meier. *Sam Bernstein*

BMW's archive service and discovered the company's classic group would give him a "zertificat" for serial #652581 for a small fee. He mailed in the paperwork and waited. He hoped the service would identify when the bike was manufactured, where it was first delivered, to whom, and what the color was when new.

Two months later, the zertificat arrived. It stated that chassis #652581 was manufactured on April 17, 1956. The R69 was one of 2,956 produced between 1955 and 1960. The bike was delivered to Georg Meier of Munich on January 2, 1957.

Normally, a name like Georg Meier would not get Bernstein excited, but he had been to the Isle of Man TT (Tourist Trophy) races a couple of years earlier, and he was quite familiar with the name. This bike had been sold to *the* Georg Meier, German motorcycle racing ace.

Meier was known as "Schorsch" when he was an apprentice in Bavaria, where he worked in a motorcycle repair shop. He showed quite well as an amateur and eventually was offered a works ride with the BMW factory racing team. He was credited as being the first rider to lap a Grand Prix track, the Spanish Spa Francorchamps circuit, at more than 100 mph.

But he received worldwide recognition when he won the senior division at the Isle of Man TT event in 1939. He averaged 89.38 mph and completed the 33-mile course in 2 hours, 57.19 seconds. He was the first foreign winner of the event.

When Bernstein visited the Isle of Man TT in 1989, it happened to be Meier's 50th anniversary of his win. Meier, now an old man, made a ceremonial lap of the circuit to commemorate his victory a half century earlier.

"When I got the zertificat, I immediately recognized the name," he said. "He was the greatest German motorcycle racer ever. This just blew me away, it was so unexpected. I had actually met him in the paddock, but I was only vaguely familiar with him at the time."

After World War II, Meier returned to racing and actually won the German 500cc Championship on a supercharged BMW six out of the seven times he entered. Upon retiring from racing in the 1950s, Meier opened a successful BMW dealership in Munich.

"So serial #652581 was shipped to Georg Meier in early 1957, nearly 20 years after his TT win," said Bernstein. "As to whether he personally owned the bike or it was for resale, I can't say. But the records list him as the first owner of the bike."

Bernstein was thrilled. He had purchased a cool-looking BMW bobber with the intention of restoring it, but fell in love with another bike and swapped. The bike he took on was a restoration project that required a bit of imagination to envision as a completed bike. And like any good fairytale, one "kiss" from Bernstein's wallet turned an ugly frog into a show-winning prince—one with a terrific history.

"My feeling is there is something magical about taking a motorcycle that is rusted and bent, and re-creating it to a like-new condition," he said. "I'm not mechanically inclined, but there is magic in the ability to do that. My feeling is that if we don't restore these old bikes for our generation, who will do it in the future? It would have been a tragedy for this thing to have languished as a rusted frame and engine case, just sitting on someone's garage floor."

Bernstein owned the R69 for about 14 months, but as he said, he's a project guy.

"I like to get into an area, learn about it, challenge myself, and do a project such as restoring the R69," he said. "To me, the process is the journey. When it's done, I like to move on to another challenge."

He has since sold his R69 to a German enthusiast in Santa Rosa, California, who also knew who Georg Meier was. His next project, a 1947 Harley-Davidson Knucklehead bobber, was recently completed and just sold to the owner of a bar in Hungary.

"I've been a rider for 45 years," he said. "It takes a lot of financial commitment and emotional energy to part with this kind of quality restoration. But it's the way I've always done it."

A COLLAPSED BARN FIND
by John Casteras

Of the motorcycles my wife Nancy and I have restored, our 1905 Indian was probably the least likely candidate for a new life when it was discovered beneath the rubble of a barn that collapsed about the time of the Great Depression.

We came into the bike hobby through our shared interests in old British cars. I had bought a 1952 MG TD when I was in college and rebuilt it, and, as a married couple, Nancy and I did the same to a 1959 MGA coupe. After restoring the MGA, we were looking for a new project and thought maybe something lighter that took up less room would be attractive, so around 1975 I started looking into what was available in the vintage motorcycle field.

I found there were old bikes to be had, but it wasn't like buying stuff for the MGs, where I could just go to a catalog and order parts. Back then, a fellow really had to make contacts and study; there weren't many books out on this topic.

My father-in-law provided the inspiration that led us to our first two-wheeled project. He gave us an Indian engine he had received in trade for digging a well back in the 1930s. The guy he did the work for went out of business and traded him some stuff he had around his shop.

John and Nancy Casteras have turned a nearly gone 1905 Indian barn find into a complete motorcycle. The silver canister in front of the head is the carburetor. Wheels are wrapped with 2x28-inch U.S. Rubber Co. tires.

213

The engine was a circa-1920 racing unit that had been in a Troy, New York, Indian dealership. It turned out to be a Daytona engine that had last been installed in a hill-climber.

From there, we had to find a frame and other parts to build a bike around this rare and special engine. Our search taught us that everything we needed to build a historic bike was out there, but it was only through our contacts that we were able to find it. We dug ourselves deeper into this hobby because our parts search opened the doors to other automotive restoration projects we wanted to do.

I was able to find a 1918 Indian cradle frame to complement the Daytona engine, and we were happy with that combination until five years ago, when I found somebody who was reproducing a correct Daytona frame. We took the Daytona engine out of its cradle frame and installed it in the proper Daytona frame and located a stock engine for the '18 project. Now, from that one bike came two: the 1918 Powerplus and the circa-1920 Daytona racer.

That's how we got into antique motorcycles. Now, for the collapsed barn story.

1905 Indian

In the 1970s, Margaret, who lived in Peekskill, New York, heard that a co-worker's relative had an early motorcycle stored on a farm in Connecticut. She jumped at the chance to secure the bike for her husband as a surprise.

The surprise was on her as the barn sheltering the bike had collapsed during a nor'easter in the 1930s, and no one had been motivated to retrieve it in 40 years. The couple had to dig through the rubble to free what they discovered to be a 1905 Indian "motocycle"—that's how Indian literature from the period spelled it—in terrible condition.

To document the occasion, they leaned the remains against a shed and took some black-and-white photos. Casualties from decades of damp entombment included a banged-up headlight, half of a front fork, a missing front wheel, a nearly spokeless rear wheel, and a chain that had rusted solid.

It was wearing Indian's torpedo-like gas tank on the top frame tube, which was period-correct but not the way it came from the factory in 1905. The 13-cid (213cc) single-cylinder engine produced $1^3/4$ horsepower in its day and was largely intact.

This barn find was missing the tube that housed the three-cell battery pack for the coil ignition, which Indian claimed was good for 800 to 2,500 miles before replacement. These were actually Indian-specific batteries made by Thomas Edison's company.

Here is the Indian just moments after it was dug out from under the collapsed barn in Connecticut. It might not look like much, but the essentials are intact, including the diamond frame and single-cylinder engine.

Ninety-nine percent of the people finding this 1905 Indian in the remains of a collapsed building would toss it in the scrap pile with all of the other rusted machine parts. Knowing what to look for is the difference between being a junk collector and a preserver of historic motorcycles.

This bike is Roosevelt-era vintage—Theodore, not Franklin!

The handlebars' twist grip controls were partly there but very rusted, and there was no trace of the advertised blue, black, red, or green factory colors.

Back in 1905, $210 bought five troy ounces of gold or a new Indian motorcycle. Architecture for the Indian was a standard bicycle frame, what they called a "diamond frame," owing to the shape the tubes make when viewed in profile. It had a hanger for the cranks, which enabled you to get the bike rolling with a pedal start. The chain on the right starts the rear wheel going, and that drives the engine. Once the engine is turning, the rider engages the ignition. The seat post has a special kind of nut that threads into the cylinder head, so the rearward-leaning engine becomes a stressed member of the frame.

When new, a canister at the bottom of the frame served as the muffler. The single's intake was atmospheric, with the suction of the engine opening the valve and drawing in the air-fuel mixture. The exhaust valve was on the right side of the block. Lubrication was by way of a small glass oil-filled reservoir behind the engine. There was no pump; oil was meant to drip into the crankcase.

Early bikes were often fitted with a carbide-based headlight system. Calcium carbide was stored in a reservoir on the frame and mixed with water to produce acetylene gas. The gas passed through a rubber tube to the headlight. A mirror behind the burner was meant to amplify and project the light, but I imagine that beam was about as powerful as holding up a match at nighttime. It was more for the purpose of being seen than of seeing.

Margaret purchased that wreck of an Indian, and the two of them worked on finding missing pieces for it. It was an ongoing project that looked much better but was still incomplete when I bought it from them 25 years ago. Over the next five years or so, I was able to copy, make, conserve, or find the remaining items, so that the bike, while rough, looks as you see it now in the photos.

The bike now has a "camelback" gas tank rather than the torpedo-style it was wearing when rescued from the barn. I still have the torpedo tank, but a camelback tank from another source was available, and I elected to use it.

Back when I worked on the Daytona race bike, I realized I would have to make some of the missing and unavailable components. If I have an original, I can copy the thing in my own workshop. I was a research metallurgist and worked for two different outfits. Now, I'm doing stuff at home in the basement with machine tools I've acquired over the years. My own projects take precedence, but I make a lot of stuff for some other people. That's pretty much what I do now—make pieces for others' projects.

The '05 Indian's original coil is still hot and throws out quite a spark, although new leads had to be soldered to the broken ends. I made the muffler by copying an original. The engine runs, but I have no plans to ride the bike, owing to the fragility of the frame. I don't plan to fix the frame; I kind of like the bike as is.

This front ¾-angle picture shows how severe the deterioration was on the '05 Indian. The front fork has literally rotted from the ground up. There's no doubt this bike was a sponge for moisture for the four decades it lay on the ground.

When we got into this hobby, the trend was to take barn finds and beautiful original-paint bikes and restore them to original or "better" condition with chrome and paint they didn't come with. My plan is to keep the '05 intact with its historic rust in place.

The Rest of the Collection

Getting that Daytona engine from Nancy's father put us on a path that brought more and more bikes to our door. I have a 1931 Indian 101 Scout that only needed some magneto work and a few other things. It was exported to Sweden in the 1930s and came back to the States around 1994.

Margaret's brother-in-law had a 1913 Indian I acquired that will someday need assembling. He also had a BSA Bantam, into which somebody who worked for Indian had

Former career metallurgist John Casteras likes the engineering behind his Belgian-built FN motorcycle because he says, "The parts fit together very precisely, like gun parts." It's probably no coincidence that FN, or Fabrique Nationale, is a gun manufacturer.

installed a 1912 engine, just for fun. I got that along with the '13 project. Nancy bought a 1949 Indian Scout 249 "vertical" around 1990. We've restored that, and it's a runner.

My favorite bike is probably our 1907 Fabrique Nationale (FN). FN is a huge firearms manufacturer founded in Herstal, Belgium, that started making motorcycles in 1889. The company built the first four-cylinder motorcycle with shaft drive and magneto ignitions in 1905, and that setup served as the basis for the U.S.-made Pierce four-cylinders that came a little later. For many years, Earle Ovington sold FN products out of New York City and Boston, so they are well known among American collectors. Mine was found in St. Paul, Minnesota, missing its fork, frame, gas tank, exhaust, and many other bits.

I saw one in Copenhagen in 1966 on the street, and it sounded like a sewing machine. I thought it was the most wonderful thing I had ever seen. It would be another 30 or 40 years before I could find one. I had to make a frame and a fork for it, as well as many other things, but it now looks like a motorcycle.

THE WORLD'S FASTEST INDIAN

How does it feel to be the keeper of the most famous motorcycle in the world?

Ask Tom Hensley. His family has owned Burt Munro's Indian streamliner since way before it became famous. Hensley manages the bike as part of a small motorcycle collection for the family, in honor not only of Munro, but also for Hensley's late brother, Dean.

First about Munro. If you haven't seen the 2005 movie *The World's Fastest Indian*, starring Anthony Hopkins, set aside your next available evening and rent the movie. To anyone interested enough to leaf through a book titled *The Harley in the Barn*, the movie is a must-see.

Munro was born in Invercargill, New Zealand, in 1899, and from childhood was interested in all things mechanical: cars, trucks, airplanes, boats, and motorcycles. Living on his family's farm did not give him much opportunity to see many vehicles. Growing up in a remote area, though, did teach him that he needed to be self-sufficient: he sometimes had to build parts from scratch if he wanted to get a job done.

In 1920, as a 21-year-old, Munro purchased a brand-new Indian Scout motorcycle, which had a 600cc engine and a top speed of 55 mph. This modest

It's hard to believe that at one time, this was a stock Indian Scout. Munro burned up speedways in his native New Zealand in the late 1930s and 1940s before setting his sights on land speed records. *Photos from Petersen Publishing Company Courtesy of Hensley Family Collection*

Fully clothed, this is what Munro's Indian looked like with its fiberglass bodywork in place. Munro stands in the middle without a hat, surrounded by his all-volunteer crew.
Photos from Petersen Publishing Company Courtesy of Hensley Family Collection

speed only kept the young man intrigued for so long, and by 1926, he had already begun modifying the bike.

His prowess in modifying and riding bikes won some acclaim. At one point he competed in professional Speedway races and eventually set seven New Zealand speed records, beginning in 1938.

Munro set his sights on a land speed record, and traveled to the Bonneville Salt Flats in Utah, for the annual Speedweeks trials to investigate the scene and plan his strategy.

He continued to modify his bike, and in 1962, with its engine punched out from 600cc to 800cc, Munro set a record of 178.95 mph. In 1966 he set another record.

The people who frequent Bonneville's SpeedWeeks took a liking to Munro. They knew he was broke, but they also knew he was a genius. Folks befriended him, loaned him tools, and gave him spare parts and a place to sleep.

The Pierce family was one who took Munro in. They were from San Gabriel, California, and owned Pierce Indian, one of the leading parts and service centers after the Indian factory closed its doors in 1953. During the 10 years that Munro competed at Bonneville, the Pierces allowed him to store his bike at their facility when he traveled back home to New Zealand. They also

He didn't have much money, but Munro had a spirit that drew people to help him achieve his dream of breaking the land speed record. He ultimately reached 183.586 MPH in 1967, making it the World's Fastest Indian, a record that still stands today. *Photos from Petersen Publishing Company Courtesy of Hensley Family Collection*

gave him parts and allowed him to use their shop to work on his bike prior to bringing it to Bonneville.

"The Pierces sponsored Burt in 1967, which is why the fiberglass bodywork had a 'Pierce Indian of San Gabriel' painted on the bike's tail," Hensley said. "Burt started to run on nitro when he came to the States, so every winter when he brought his engine back home to rebuild, the Pierces bottled up nitromethane in wine bottles and sent them along, because he couldn't get it in New Zealand." The nitro is also why he kept burning holes in pistons, because he was casting them himself in the backyard from probably inferior materials.

In addition to pistons, Munro made his own cylinder barrels, flywheels, and numerous other items. In fact, the hoops that supported the fiberglass body were actually recycled fence post stakes. Munro also built connecting rods out of old Ford tractor axles.

Munro's effort in 1967 seems to have brought all the lessons of the previous years together. If racing was a young-man's sport, Munro knew nothing about it; he was 68 years old and his motorcycle was 47.

By now his Indian's engine had grown to 950cc. When his turn to race finally came, he turned in a two-way average of 183.586 mph, finally breaking the under-1000cc world record.

After having been raced for a half-century, Burt Munro's famous Indian was at first displayed at a dealership in the 1970s, but eventually put out to pasture next to a storage building. This is the condition of the 1920 Scout when acquired by the late Dean Hensley in 1984. *Photos from Petersen Publishing Company Courtesy of Hensley Family Collection*

Munro ran at Bonneville a couple of more times, but he finally hung up his helmet in 1970, when he was 71 years old. When he left America for the last time, he gave his beloved Indian to the Pierce family as a thank you for all the years of assistance.

For a while the Pierces displayed the World's Fastest Indian in their showroom, then relegated it to the warehouse, and ultimately to the elements outside, where the decades of Munro's loving modifications slowly deteriorated into the ground.

Enthusiast Gordy Clark purchased the Indian from the Pierces, but just put it into storage. Remember, at this time Munro's motorcycle was just a beat-up old racer, not very interesting to even the most serious motorcycle collectors. This was before the modern antique bike craze really took off. It was a curiosity, nothing more.

Enter Dean Hensley. Dean, Tom Hensley's older brother, was a rising motorcycle racing star. At just 18 years old he was already making a name for himself on the road racing circuit. One day he was racing at the El Sonora track when he wrecked and was run over by another bike.

"When my parents got the call about my brother, I rode to the hospital with them," Tom Hensley said, 12 years old at the time. "Hell, I didn't even know what the word *paralyzed* meant. They had him in traction, but managed

Getting ready to go; Munro is about to climb into his Indian streamliner during one of his many record attempts at the Bonneville Salt Flats in Utah. *Photos from Petersen Publishing Company Courtesy of Hensley Family Collection*

to somehow drop him to the floor when he first arrived. But even though he was paralyzed from the chest down, he bounced back like a flower."

Dean Hensley and his younger brother Tom, who at 13 became his brother's full-time caregiver, went into business.

"He went to the fine art school at Pasadena City College to learn how to pinstripe and paint flames," Tom said. "One thing led to another and we began selling antique-looking mirrors that we sold to pubs." According to Tom, the mirror business was earning $2 million a year in the early 1980s.

"He had known about the Indian for years," Tom said, referring to the historic bike that had been stored in a neglected state among Gordy Clark's

300-bike collection. Dean purchased the bike in 1986, soon after selling the antique mirror company.

"He had gone to an auction, maybe it was at Hershey, and saw that old streamliners were beginning to sell for substantial money," Tom said. "That's when he decided to try and buy the old Burt Munro bike."

After the purchase, Munro's Indian sat around for a few years as Dean gathered enough information and parts to begin restoration. "The body was beaten down like nobody's business," said Tom. "As we say out here on the West Coast: it was *crusty*. We have detailed photos of the restoration. Since the bike sat outside for years, four frame tubes filled with water and rusted out."

Tom said that the photographs are proof they own the actual Indian. He said there are collectors in New Zealand who claim to own the actual World's Fastest Indian, but he said that was actually a chassis mock-up that Munro used to test his engines. Tom Hensley said Munro's bike never left the United States once it was shipped here in 1962.

Dean Hensley had the bike restored by master restorer Steve Huntsinger. The bike was never completely reassembled because Dean wanted to be able to sit on the bike at start-up. So special hand-controls were adapted and half the body was not installed.

"The left side of the body hung on my garage wall for 20 years," said brother Tom. "The fiberglass had settled, so getting it fitting back together was like fixing Marty Feldman's eyes. We had to mount it to a board, let it sit in the sun, and every day turn the set screws one-quarter turn to get the body to move back into place."

Dean brought his now-restored Indian streamliner to a Davenport, Iowa, swap meet and decided to start the bike after it hadn't run in 20 years. They had built an Indy-type starter that mounted on the countershaft, and Dean could operate it with hand controls.

"They had never de-tuned the engine, so they were still running high compression," Tom said. "My brother revved it up running on methanol and snapped a connecting rod." Afterward, the bike was relegated to a static show bike.

Sadly, Dean Hensley, who had worked so hard and accomplished so much in the worlds of art, business, and motorcycles, was killed in an auto accident in May 1992. Tom continued to show the bike after his brother's passing, but other collectors made him upset.

"What pissed me off was that I had collectors trying to buy my brother's bikes even before I could get him buried," he said. "So I said, 'You know what guys? You guys ain't getting shit.' That's why I've kept all his stuff." A big brother is a big brother—Tom keeps the bike out of love and respect for Dean.

Besides Munro's Indian, the Hensley family collection includes the original Globe of Death theatrical Indian; an original Isle of Man overhead cam prototype racer; Gene Ryan's factory overhead valve hill-climber; and the last Indian to win at Ascot Park.

Another memento from Dean is the 1958 Ford Ranchero equipped with hand controls. "I drove it just the other day," Tom said.

In the spring of 2011, Tom received a phone call from the organizers of the Pebble Beach Concours d'Elegance. They said if he could prepare the streamliner to running condition, he could enter it in the prestigious show. "We were already in the process of getting the bike running with new rods and pistons when Pebble Beach called," he said. "They said it had to be in running condition in order to come to the show, so we built brand-new cylinders from scratch and had the bodywork fitted exactly the way Munro had it mounted when he ran for the record in 1967."

By August, the bike was completed. The Pebble Beach organizers conducted a thorough analysis of the bike's restoration, making sure it was authentic before being invited to be displayed on the lawn. It was displayed at Pebble Beach with only one-half the bodywork mounted. "Once you mount the entire body, all the work and craftsmanship of the frame and engine is hidden."

Slight modifications were made so the bike could be started in the event it was invited to the trophy presentation. For instance, Munro had no carburetor venturi, making idling impossible. "It was like sucking soda through a funnel," Tom said. "It wouldn't run at low rpms."

It's a good thing Tom got the bike to operate, because it was called onto the stage for a first place trophy in the racing motorcycle category. "We started it up," he said. "My brother was the last person to run it, and almost 25 years later, I was the next."

Having won the show of all shows, the Hensley family is considering what to do next. "This is not my bike, it belongs to my family's collection," Tom is quick to point out. "I have two sisters and a brother. They have been gracious enough to help keep the collection of my brother's bikes together."

They are now considering selling the collection, which includes about a dozen bikes, as a single unit. Since New Zealanders consider Burt Munro to be their John Wayne, I'd be surprised if someone down there didn't buy it. But parting with the family collection won't be easy. Tom truly cares who owns these bikes next.

"After all, this is my brother's legacy," he said.

ULTRA CLASSIC CURSE
by Brad Bowling

A 16-year-old Harley-Davidson Ultra Classic with virtually no miles for only $2,000 sounds like the bargain of a lifetime, but David Dammen has many times regretted the day he rolled such a bike from its first owner's shed onto his trailer.

Maybe the universe punishes motorcycle enthusiasts who try to make the transition from Hondas to Harleys. Or maybe Dammen was not meant to own and enjoy a Harley-Davidson Ultra Classic motorcycle. Maybe that particular bike was cursed from the moment it left the factory, like the Plymouth Fury in the film version of Stephen King's *Christine*. No matter how one looks at the situation, Dammen definitely bit off more than he could chew.

The Minot, North Dakota, mechanic and all-around fabricator has been enjoying two-wheeled travel since his earliest homebuilt scooters. His first motorcycle was a 1960 Honda Dream 160, after which he rode a 1973 Honda 350 four-cylinder. He sold the 350 after having children, but eventually bought a Honda Custom 750.

In 1990, Dammen came dangerously close to leaving the Honda family because he wanted a new Harley-Davidson Ultra Classic. During the harsh

Sometimes your dream becomes your nightmare. David Dammen purchased this ultra-low-mileage 1990 Harley Ultra Classic for $2,000. Sometimes he wishes he had just taken a pass on the purchase. *David Dammen*

North Dakota winter he was negotiating to buy one of the company's biggest bikes, powered by a 1340cc V-twin and five-speed transmission, when the owner of the dealership died. With his momentum interrupted, Dammen waited a few years, and bought the full-dresser 1994 Honda Gold Wing Aspencade that continues to give him miles of riding pleasure. "The Ultra Classic was the fanciest thing Harley made then," Dammen said. "Even though I stayed with Honda, I always thought about that Harley."

In 2007, Dammen thought the universe was giving him another chance to own a Harley when someone he worked with asked if he would be interested in a bike whose owner had passed away. "He told me this guy had died and his wife was trying to sell his Harley," Dammen said. "My friend thought it was an '82 or '83 dresser. Buying a motorcycle that old didn't bother me because I can build whole cars. I thought it could be a fun project if the price was right. I asked if he knew what was wrong with it; he said he heard it needed some wiring work."

Dammen took down the contact phone number and called the owner's son, who told him the bike was a 1990 Ultra Classic his father had bought new. The widow was asking $8,000 for it, but the son said he would take $5,000. He warned Dammen that it wasn't in perfect condition—the headlight was missing, for example.

Dammen arranged to see the Harley and took his nephew along for an extra set of eyes. Unfortunately, it only took one good eye to spot the problems. It was intact but looked like everything on the exterior had been modified by an amateur. The factory radio had been replaced with a much cheaper unit. The paint on the fenders was puffy and cracked, as if they had been exposed to too much sunlight. A voice inside Dammen's head was screaming for him to run away, but this is a veteran mechanic whose 30x40 feet shop has enough tools, lifts, and heaters to fix anything 365 days a year. He had started building '57 Chevy hot rods when he was 16 and owned an auto repair shop for years. How much trouble could one motorcycle be?

From the son, Dammen learned that the owner had bought the Harley after retiring from the Air Force. He said his father and mother had taken many trips on the bike and really enjoyed it. The father had passed away three years earlier, and the bike had not been ridden for 10 years prior to that. For that last decade, his father had rolled it out of the garage each spring and rolled it back in each winter. Simple math told Dammen the Ultra Classic he was considering buying had only been driven three or four years at best, which made the son's claim of 12,000 miles plausible. "The son told me to make an offer, but I didn't want to go as high as he was asking," Dammen said. "I went home, thought about it, and called him back the next day.

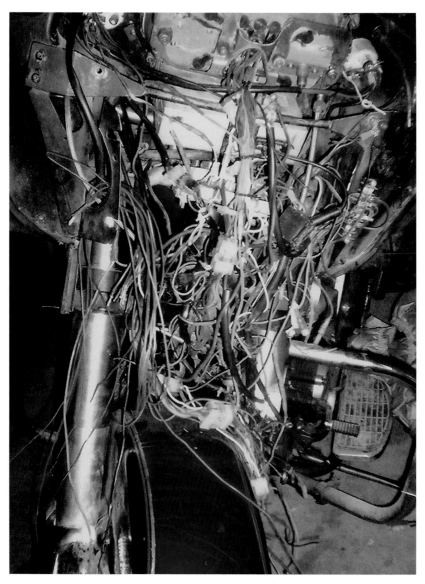

For some unknown reason, the late owner of the bike had decided to rewire the machine. He installed all-new ground wires and plug-ins, added odd connections. One four-inch wire had nine splices in it for no apparent reason. Besides the wiring, many of the nuts and bolts had been replaced with the wrong pitch threads, and others were simply stripped out. Nine Heli-Coil thread repair kits were required to repair the engine alone. *David Dammen*

"'I don't want to insult you with this offer,' I told him, 'but I really think it's worth about $2,000. There are a lot of things wrong with it.' He accepted, so there I was—another proud owner of a Harley-Davidson motorcycle."

There were no keys to the bike, so after towing it home to his shop, Dammen hotwired the ignition and fired up the big V-twin. Dammen was encouraged by the easy start and smooth rumble; once again, he thought, "How bad can it be?"

With many other projects demanding his attention, Dammen put his new Ultra Classic aside until the fall, at which point he began to discover the nightmarish nature of his purchase. Over the course of the next four years, Dammen learned that the bike's first owner had suffered the final decade of his life with an extreme form of mental illness and that every nut, bolt, and major component of the bike had been "improved" by a mechanic for whom reality was merely a vacation spot.

To say that the wiring harness was a mess is a profound understatement. Dammen discovered from the local Harley dealer that the owner bought a lot of new clips for the plugins because he claimed they "went bad" every year and had to be replaced. What the guys at the parts counter did not know is that the '90 Ultra Classic's nervous system looked like a middle school science project gone haywire. The owner put in splices, odd connections, and wires that ran to nowhere. He ran so many wires from the tail-lamp that it was necessary to cut a larger hole in the rear fender so the wad of insulated copper could pass through to the fusebox. Instead of allowing bulbs and other components to function from the factory ground wires, the owner gave each part individual grounds.

"I had to buy all of the wiring and switches for the handlebars," Dammen said. "He had cut the wires off flush with the switch, then dug plastic off behind the switch and soldered new wire onto it." The parts could not be repaired.

"The craziest thing I've seen is one of the gauges—the one by the right-hand side of the dash—has a ground wire that comes out for the dash light that runs to a common ground. He had spliced that four-inch wire in four places for no reason I could see."

Because there were no keys, Dammen had to replace the ignition switch, which would ordinarily be easy for such an accomplished mechanic. "Not so fast," said the Harley from hell. Dammen's contacts at the Harley dealer told him to find the pin that would release the switch from its housing, but Dammen couldn't see it. He finally realized the first owner had wrapped the switch in fiberglass resin. Also, in place of the missing headlight was a gob of spliced-on wires sticking out of the top of the fork, and they were all the same color.

Repairing the electrical system, though, was a cakewalk compared to the engine.

"The side cover was loose and there was sand in the cam box," Dammen said. "I don't know how that got in there but it made me tear everything apart, and I'm glad I did.

"The bolts that hold the rocker arms in place had been driven in by force. You could see on the bolt heads where they had been pounded in with a metal hammer. He replaced a lot of the factory bolts in the engine with finer or wrong-size threads, so everything had been stripped out. I had to put nine Heli-Coil thread repair kits into the engine alone." The oil pump had the wrong gears installed and was torqued so tight that the pump would not move.

On the frame, the owner had drilled the threads out of the welded-on nuts and put separate nuts behind them. The rear tire was installed backward, so Dammen pulled it and noticed there was an innertube—a truck innertube—inside the tire. The tube was so large that the owner had simply folded the excess and stuffed it into the tire.

The Harley factory radio had been removed and replaced with a cheap unit, which would not have been so awful had he not used a reciprocating saw to cut the larger hole in the console. Generous helpings of epoxy held the new radio in place. The CB radio and other electronics were missing; covering the openings were some glued-on strips of leather. Clear paint and fiberglass resin were so thick on the front fender—in some spots as high as a quarter inch—that Dammen had to use a chisel to scrape it off. Underneath lay a perfect fender.

No detail was too small to escape the many "improvements" the first owner forced on the poor Harley. For instance, with great precision, the owner stripped every tooth from the speedometer gear. He sawed the pin off the kickstand where the return spring attaches and installed a screw further back so the stand just dangled from the bottom of the undercarriage.

At some point during his time with a new Harley Ultra Classic, the first owner must have heard that the front suspension could be stiffened for very little money by simply putting plastic spacers above the factory springs. Dammen was not surprised to find segments of plastic water pipe when he dismantled the forks. "Here's the most impressive thing," Dammen said. "I mean, this took some ingenuity on his part, which is why I think he was probably an adequate mechanic but that something was not right in his brain.

"He managed to change the throttle grip on the handlebars so it had to be rotated *forward* to increase engine speed. Changing that required a lot of engineering with the cable because it was never meant to work that way. However, in doing so, he broke the cable mountings on the carburetors."

For four years, Dammen has worked on the '90 Harley in two- to three-month spurts. As of this writing, his project is less than six months away

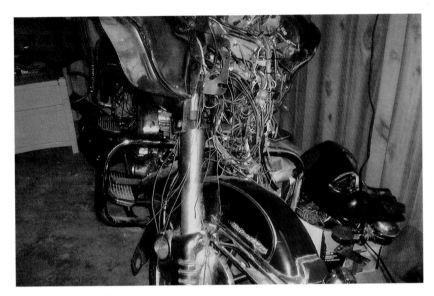

What a mess! *David Dammen*

from completion. His family gave him a wiring harness for Christmas. He has stripped and repaired the frame, rebuilt the engine with fresh seals and bearings, replaced cross-threaded bolts with new bolts and threads, and located all of the missing components. The gas tank and both fenders have been finished, primed, and are awaiting fresh paint. Dammen hopes he has exorcised the bike of its curse.

"One other thing amazes me about this bike and the story behind it," Dammen said. "When I had the engine apart, I saw that the cylinder walls still had the factory crosshatch pattern. I don't know who came up with the 12,000-mile estimate, but this engine never reached its break-in mileage. I doubt it traveled more than a few hundred miles at most!"

Dammen feels bad for the Harley's previous owner, who was obviously dealing with severe mental problems toward the end of his life, but he admits his patience for the project waned the longer he worked on it.

"I've never seen anything like this," Dammen said. "It was crazy how many ways he found to mess up this bike. Every single part was ruined in some way during the 13 years he had it. Even though it's made me mad for the last four years, I don't mind telling people about it. I would probably laugh at this story if it were happening to someone else."

THE CONSOLATION PRIZE

"You can't always get what you want," advises the Rolling Stones' classic tune, but Mick Jagger tells us that sometimes we get what we need. The sentiment perfectly describes how John Brutosky's 1967 Harley-Davidson FLH Electra Glide came to be in his collection of original-paint Milwaukee-built motorcycles.

Brutosky, now retired from the City of Passaic, New Jersey, Fire Department, had been actively pursuing vintage Harleys for three decades when he found the '67 in a chicken coop. "I was bitten by the Harley bug in 1978," the former lieutenant said, "when I bought my first one. It was an original-paint 1948 Panhead that I got for $1,600, which was a lot of money back then. I only paid so much because it was such a nice original bike."

Since putting that first example of the Milwaukee Marvel into his garage, Brutosky was motivated to find others. The firefighter's work schedule gave him enormous flexibility for hunting and buying bikes—24 hours on duty followed by 72 hours off.

Harley's top model achieved legendary pop culture status with 1973's *Electra Glide in Blue*, an anti-establishment film starring Robert Blake as a motorcycle officer in Arizona. "He's a good cop on a big bike on a bad road" barked the promotional poster. John Brutosky's '67 Electra Glide, which was living in a chicken coop in Gary, Indiana, when he bought it, featured this unusual white banana-style seat.

"My '48 is what got me hooked on original-paint bikes," Brutosky said. "I knew going into it that collecting unrestored vintage motorcycles in good condition was a really hard goal for anyone to meet. Some guys will buy a restored bike for their collection, then sell off the restored model when they find an original-paint example of the same bike. That's how strong the allure of original-paint bikes is."

By 2004, his original-paint Harley collection numbered 14 bikes covering years 1936–1939 and 1946–1949, a couple of other Shovelheads and Panheads, and a '56. Then he heard about a '68 Electra Glide in Radcliff, Kentucky. "I was living in Haledon, New Jersey, when I heard there was an estate auction selling a '68 with only 400 miles on it," Brutosky said. "I got off work and drove two days to get there.

"When I arrived, they let me inspect the bike but I was discouraged right away because there were some heavy hitters swarming around it, including some folks from a well-known collector's entourage. I can't compete with those big guys. They can spend $50,000 on a bike and write it off as a charitable expense. My collection was built on finding bargains that somehow stayed under everybody's radar."

Disappointed but still in the mood for some Harley hunting, Brutosky called a friend in Indiana to see if he had any leads to share. The friend told him there was a '67 Electra Glide in Gary that might be for sale by the original owner but that it had been stored for many years in an old chicken coop. That news was all it took for Brutosky to point his truck northwest and beat it to Gary. "My friend wasn't interested in the bike," he said. "Maybe its storage location turned him off, but I met with the old-timer who had had it since new and we worked out a deal. I got it dirt cheap."

The Electra Glide, so named since its introduction in 1965 for its electric starter and soft hydraulic dampers, featured the company's stout 1208cc (74ci) air-cooled V-twin engine, four-speed "ratchet top" transmission, the finger-catching "mousetrap" clutch mechanism (in its final year), hydraulic rear brakes, hard luggage, windscreen, turn signals, and a custom two-tone paint scheme that beautifully combined Harley's Hi-Fi Blue with White. The bike had been ordered to its first owner's taste, which included a rare banana-style seat in place of the standard spring-mounted rider's perch. Lighter Sportster models were often fitted with the banana seat, but it was unusual to see one on the highline Electra Glide.

"It hadn't been run for 12 years when I saw it, and it only had 12,000 miles on the odometer. The tires were actually so dry-rotted and flat—and the rear brake was locked up—that we couldn't push it out of the coop."

Since a fully dressed Electra Glide tops 500 pounds, it was no easy task transplanting it onto his truck, but a group of four strong locals managed to

John Brutosky's attention has turned away from Harley-Davidson motorcycles in the past few years. He now pursues and restores Indian Fours.

lift it into the bed. Although complete and in decent condition, the '67 needed a lot of elbow grease when Brutosky got it back to New Jersey.

The Harley enthusiast pulled the oil and gas tanks, flushing out their clogged, decade-old fluids. He removed the clutch and primary chain, performed a total brake job, installed new tires, and rewired a few parts suffering from dry rot. With some fresh fuel and lube, the Electra Glide roared back to life.

"It had a Tillotson carburetor that was a real nightmare to rebuild," Brutosky said. "They are hard to set up, and you really have to know how to tweak them. They are good carbs when you get them right, but Harley phased them out because a lot of guys had problems with them."

As for restoring the shine of the precious Hi-Fi Blue and White paint, Brutosky's secret is nothing more than soap and water. "The paint actually looked pretty good," he said. "The '67 looked like a barn bike when I found it, so there was a lot of rust and crust on it. The outside of the engine needed cleaning. I just blew that stuff off, hosed it off, and blew the dust off. After that, I rode it just the way it came out of the coop. Pigeon droppings had damaged

234

the paint on my '48 Harley, which suffered from being stored outside, but the '67 cleaned up well."

Like all collectors, Brutosky is always pursuing his next must-have discovery, which eventually led to the '67 Electra Glide and several other bikes going to new owners. During the past four years, the former fireman has found a new outlet for his two-wheeled enthusiasm. "I was a Harley guy my whole life until I met an old-timer who was into Indian Fours, which are a whole different animal," Brutosky said.

Since then, he has devoted himself to finding and restoring the Springfield, Massachusetts–built four-cylinder beauties that were last produced in 1942.

"Indians are very time consuming," Brutosky said. "You can probably do 10 Harley motors by the time you do one of the Fours. You have to make up a lot of your own bushings. I spent months making up jigs to pour my own Babbitt metal and machine it all to crank size."

So far, Brutosky reports he has found no Indian Fours in chicken coops.

THE MYSTERY OF THE HIDDEN HARLEY
by Brad Bowling

In the case of Steve Barber's 1957 Harley-Davidson FLH, the traditional barn-find story takes a twist worthy of an Edgar Allan Poe thriller—in fact, it reads a lot like Poe's 1846 short story, "The Cask of Amontillado." Poe's super-creepy tale of a nobleman who kills a deceptive friend by building a stone wall around him in his dungeon has scared many a high school sophomore, but we do not know if the Harley's first owner drew inspiration from that plot or acted on his own.

What *is* documented is that "Hank" was a successful Pittsburgh businessman when he bought a fully loaded '57 FLH. As if having the "Cadillac of motorcycles" wasn't enough, Hank fired a stream of dollars into the Harley dealership's parts department, which hung every accessory imaginable on the big cruiser, including Harley's King of the Highway package, a wide-whitewall Goodyear front tire, Big Bertha saddlebags, Super Soft DeLuxe Buddy seat, Guide DH-49 turn signal kit, lots of extra chrome, and some aftermarket pieces from Beck, Buco, and Superior. Hank's free-

This 1957 Harley-Davidson came out of its long, lonely storage looking just like this. The motive behind its secret entombment has been lost to history, but the bike is a museum piece the likes of which will never be found again.

spending lifestyle included a weekend home in the undeveloped mountains near Pittsburgh, which explains the Harley's rear Goodyear Grasshopper—a knobby dirt bike tire not usually mounted on high-dollar cruisers.

Out the door, Hank's clack-and-pepper red ride was one of the most expensive Harley-Davidson products sold that year. Since very little information about the owner is available, it is possible Hank's spending spree was an attempt to outgun a singer/movie star from Tupelo, Mississippi, who was the most famous Harley rider of that era—Elvis. Elvis Presley's anti-establishment image had recently been bolstered by widely circulated photos of the hipster and his Black '57 FLH; maybe Hank wanted to bring some two-wheeled rock 'n' roll glamour to western Pennsylvania.

With such a magnificent machine in the garage, Hank and Fay (his wife or girlfriend) were ready for many thousands of miles of travel pleasure, but something changed their plans; just as the FLH's odometer reached 247 miles—not even past the 74ci V-twin's break-in distance—Hank's attitude about his bike took on a dark and macabre tone.

For reasons he took to the grave, Hank decided to permanently park his '57 FLH. He wasn't interested in selling it, but he decided to hide it in a place where no one would find it during his lifetime, and it is unknown whether

All we know about the original owner of this '57 FLH comes from a few comments his niece/estate executor made, and from the contents of the bike's saddlebags. The Harley brand cap tells us his name was Hank, his girlfriend or wife was Fay, and he felt manly enough to wear a pink-and-white satiny western-style shirt as he rode 247 miles.

The strongest theory as to why Hank walled up his brand-new Harley lies with the transmission. When the Barber family purchased this pristine collector's item in 1993, the bike had a stuck gear. Current owner Steve Barber wonders if that condition happened in 1957 and sent Hank over the edge, or if it was simply the result of being parked for 35-plus years.

Fay knew the bike's final location. He prepared the bike for its entombment by packing the left saddlebag with his personal riding effects: a pink-and-white satin western-style riding shirt; a Harley-Davidson hat with his name painted on it; rain gear; hand cleaner; shop rags; and sunglasses. He put Fay's travel togs in the right saddlebag and an Amoco gas station road atlas of Pennsylvania in the windshield bag.

With the Hydra Glide prepped for a long road trip it would never take, Hank built around it an undetectable cedar-lined sarcophagus in his garage,

By now, this 55-year-old Harley-Davidson should have spun that odometer at least once. Instead, it froze at 247 miles until Steve Barber fired it up and rode it 40 miles in 2010.

Nothing but the best (and expensive) was fitted to the rear of this '57 Harley.

where it sat in darkness for almost 35 years. There were no windows, but the air was climate-controlled.

Unlike the victim in Poe's nightmarish narrative, the bike was eventually rescued none the worse for wear. Hank's niece inherited the property after his death and noticed the garage was slightly smaller than the original blueprints suggested. In 1993, her curiosity compelled her to investigate. Down came the secret wall, revealing the greatest archaeological surprise since King Tut was unearthed in 1922. Hank's niece transported the bike back to her home in Connecticut and placed an ad for a like-new '57 FLH in a local pennysaver newspaper.

"A friend of my father's called to tell him about the ad," Steve Barber said, whose father Joe and mother Peg had been running The 74 Shop—a Harley restoration business—in Saugerties, New York, since 1973. "Everybody who saw the ad thought the bike had been restored—that there was no pristine original out there with so few miles. It just sounded too good to be true."

Once the Barbers showed serious interest in purchasing the bike, Hank's niece/estate executor told them the bike's unusual story. The seller did not know, however, what had caused her uncle to take leave of his senses and wall up a perfectly good motorcycle.

Even Elvis didn't get this carried away. Hank had his dealer install everything Harley had in its catalog as well as aftermarket parts on his '57 FLH. It was likely one of the most expensive bikes Harley sold that year.

Steve's parents were blown away by the find. "Joe and I were overcome with joy at the sight of this brand-new 1957 Panhead," Peg said. "It was better than we could have ever dreamed."

"It was so perfect and such a time capsule for that period," Steve said, "that we decided not to try to crank it right away. It had one flaw, which is that it was stuck in gear. We've wondered if that happened back in 1957, causing Hank to get mad at the bike, or if the transmission stuck while it was put away."

Joe Barber passed away in 1996, and Peg ran The 74 Shop until 2006, when Steve took over the business. The '57 enjoyed its new life as a pampered museum piece until June 2010, when Barber resuscitated the big V-twin. He cranked the bike at the Antique Motorcycle Club of America's Rhinebeck (New York) Grand National Super Meet before a huge crowd. It was the first time anyone outside Barber's family and friends had heard the '57 fire up since it was new. A few days after the Rhinebeck show, he drove it 40 miles. Barber's plan is to take it out on rare occasions, but it will never see the thousands of miles Hank and Fay prepared it for.

"It was the best 40 miles of riding I've ever done," he said. "It was like riding 63 years into the past."

That's not entirely true. If it were a real time machine, the young Barber could drive to rural Pennsylvania, find Hank working on his secret motorcycle tomb, and solve the mystery of the phantom bike.

THE PAPER DISCOVERY
by Michael FitzSimons

Great discoveries of important bikes are not always accompanied by stinging insects, the smells of barnyard animals, and clouds of ancient dust. Sometimes it is the motorcycle's history—its pedigree, its provenance—that waits to be revealed long after the machine comes into public view.

Such was the case with the jewel of my Brough Superior collection—a not-quite-standard SS 100 that turned out to be the legendary model's prototype.

I have been riding motorcycles since I was a 10-year-old boy in Detroit. One of my earliest bikes was a British-built Ariel with a 350cc single-cylinder engine. The light chassis and easy handling of the British bikes, when compared to their heavier American contemporaries, made me an active British motorcycle enthusiast during and after my years as a University of Michigan mechanical engineering student.

When the British bike industry collapsed in the early 1970s, I could no longer enjoy new models, so I began pursuing the older ones. My training as an engineer drew me to the Vincents, which were incredibly fast, well-made machines, several of which I owned in the days when they were just gaining recognition among collectors.

Although it was in restored condition when he bought it, Michael FitzSimons has had this prototype Brough SS 100 restored to his liking since it entered his collection of rare and historic motorcycles.

But it was George Brough's Nottingham-made superbikes that eventually grabbed my attention. Brough was a second-generation motorcycle builder, racer, and designer who announced his appropriately named Superior line in 1919 and released three Mark I models to the public in 1920 (records from the early years are a subject of much debate, even within the Brough Superior Club; at least one '21 bike, an overhead-valve model, is extant). Equipped with the J.A. Prestwich & Co. side-valve V-twin powerplants, the bikes guaranteed an output of eight horsepower and a speed range of 8 to 80 miles per hour in the top gear of the Sturmey-Archer three-speed transmission.

At £175 for that first Mark I standard model to £210 for a "sporting combination" with sidecar, the first bikes were not cheap, but the public and media were impressed with the Brough's styling, power, and reliability. In 1922, a year that saw Brough Superior production jump to 103 units, George Brough earned marketing gold by piloting a side-valve motorcycle to 100 mph around the Brooklands race course in Surrey. *The Motor Cycle* magazine dubbed George Brough's creations the "Rolls-Royce of motorcycles."

In 1923, Brough introduced its SS 80, featuring a 988cc J.A. Prestwich (JAP) engine and three-speed Sturmey-Archer gearbox. Fuel efficiency was rated at 80 miles per gallon, and the factory Dunlop tires were good for 8,000 miles. The new frame was so compact and well balanced that the company boasted in its literature as one of "seven SS 80 facts" that the SS 80 could be ridden at 60 mph without touching the handlebars. (Rest assured that the seven world speed records Brough shattered that year were accomplished with the rider's hands safely on the controls). Sales of the Mark I and SS 80 ended the year at a respectable 119.

In 1924, the SS 80 received a stronger frame to handle the returning JAP V-twin. More acclaim on the race track, including a 123 mph run in competition by racer H. Le Vack on a modified SS 80, pushed production to 195 units.

Alongside the SS 80 for 1925 ran Brough's new SS 100. The 100's top speed of 100 mph was certified with each and every purchase. Based heavily on Le Vack's race-winning machine, the SS 100 featured JAP overhead-valve, twin-camshaft 998cc V-twin engines with hemispherical heads. The ride was improved by George Brough's use of a Harley-like front fork he marketed under the Castle Fork and Accessory Co.

The SS 100 was Brough's idea of the ultimate motorcycle, one that successfully combined an incredible top speed with amazing handling. It was also a beautiful design, broken down to only the most essential lines and elements. The SS 100's reputation and accomplishments cast a giant shadow over the competition, and it would stand in many ways as the company's most successful model.

Over its official production lifetime from 1925 to 1939, the SS 100 was available with either the JAP V-twin or a later (1936–1940) Matchless design. Brough made 281 of the former and 102 of the latter.

I have owned one of virtually every Brough model but became fixated on the SS 100 toward the latter part of my collecting career. I began my SS 100 infatuation with the late 1930s-era models. They were interesting, and produced at a time when George Brough was older and more settled. He was marketing the Matchless-equipped SS 100 as a sport touring model, whereas the early JAP bikes were outright superbike café racers.

Even though I've owned several of them, it still amazes me that somebody could make a bike go 100 mph in the 1920s. The tires were poor by today's standards. The gas was weak and inconsistent, as was the oil. Roads ranged in condition from mediocre to nonexistent. Every time I read about a 100-mph run, I wonder, "Where would you have done such a thing back then, except on a really large race track? And who had the nerve to do it?" Such questions make me marvel at how innovative and advanced George Brough's motorcycles were for their day.

Brough motorcycles were never imported into America when new, but their notoriety certainly reached these shores. Many British royalty owned them, as did well-known speed merchants. Lawrence of Arabia was probably the most famous Brough enthusiast. He owned eight of them, and a ninth was being built when he wrecked the eighth and died. Each of his bikes was named George, I through VIII.

After the SS 100, Brough failed to develop a significant replacement, although with a restlessness that characterizes most geniuses, he tried his hand at V-4, transverse-twin, and straight-four formats. In 1938, he turned out a pair of shaft-driven Golden Dream motorcycles with opposed four-cylinders, the likes of which the world would not see again until Honda's Gold Wing debuted as a 1975 model. He even produced 85 cars between 1935 and 1939 with Hudson engines and chassis. None of these efforts resulted in commercial success, and the company closed its doors in 1940.

Being involved in the Brough Superior Club, I knew of a very unusual SS 100 that had been restored and was in a member's collection. Its frame, which was different from all the production SS 100s I had ever seen, had "001" stamped on it, and its JAP V-twin was marked as "30726"—the lowest recorded number of JAP's 998cc engine series. The frame looked very much like an SS 80 unit that had been modified to accept the larger engine. There were, for example, lugs on the frame where an SS 80 exhaust might attach but which would have been absent on the SS 100. The forks ('24 Harley pieces), gearbox, and seat were also different from what I had seen on production versions. These facts suggested a pre-production prototype—the Holy Grail

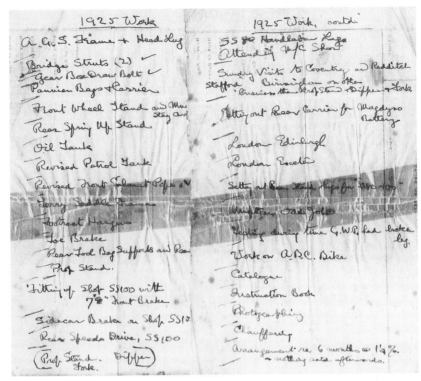

Brough's talented engineer, Harold Karslake, kept many notes on his daily activities in the shop. It was on these pages that the current owner of the 1924 SS 100 prototype found reference to his motorcycle. Until that moment, according to FitzSimons, the bike was "just this amorphous thing that didn't really exist until it was sold in 1930."

of all car/bike finds—but there was no mention of such a machine before 001 was sold to the public in 1930.

In 1986, my curiosity about this oddity got the better of me, so I bought the 001 SS 100 and spent the next decade tracing its steps back into history. I visited the National Motor Museum on Lord Montague's Beaulieu estate in the south of England and did a lot of research. In addition to the world-famous "autojumble" held each year on the grounds, the estate is home to a giant motoring library. The archives held copies of *The Motor Cycle* and *Motorcycling* magazines from the period, where I saw photos of and read about my bike. I also located images of it mocked up for beauty shots before it was quite ready for the public. There were, for example, pictures of it with wooden dowels standing in for the exhaust pipes, which would be retouched for the press to look like the real thing.

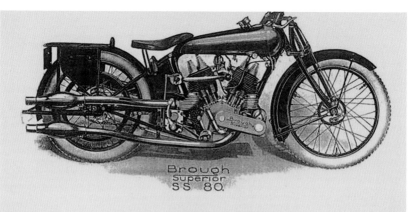

Brough
Superior
S S 80.

FULL SPECIFICATION.

ENGINE.—This is a production of the famous house of J. A. Prestwich & Co., and is specially manufactured for the "Brough Superior." The finish of all parts inside and out is superfine. Two cylinders, V type, bore 85·5 m/m., stroke 86 m/m., cubic capacity 988. It has roller bearings to big ends and main shaft. The pistons are an aluminium alloy. The Valves are a special chrome-vanadium, and are indestructible. Two return springs are fitted to each valve. Large aluminium heat dissipators are fitted in place of the usual heavy metal valve caps. The sparking plugs are fitted at an angle across the inlet valve, and it is practically impossible to oil up the plug. Two main leads are fitted, one to the rear portion of front cylinder, and a second lead to the timing case. The timing gear, although designed for speed, is practically noiseless. Each engine before being passed for fitting in its frame undergoes a very strenuous test on the bench, such a test that no superficial tuning is necessary for the complete machine to substantiate its 80 m.p.h. guarantee. **The Cylinders can be lifted for decarbonizing with the engine** *in situ*.

The balance of this Special Super Engine is such that
no vibration is appreciable at any engine speed.

The Exhaust arrangements consist of 2 long exhaust pipes 1⅜" diameter, attached to streamlined and ribbed Aluminium heat dissipators attached to Engine. The pipes are carried to the rear of machine, and there are attached two streamlined Aluminium Silencers of protected design. **The exhaust is really silenced.**

FRAME.—Second only in importance to the Engine for such a speedy machine as the "SS 80" is the Frame. Half the pleasure in speeding is the feeling of confidence, due to perfect steering and balance. It is a fact that the "SS 80" can be ridden "hands off" at 60 m.p.h. A glance at the illustration will show that the Frame is the neatest, and houses its appurtenances in a more compact manner than any frame on the market. Cylinders can be dismantled without taking crankcase out of frame. The minimum ground clearance is 4¾", yet the saddle height is 27" only. All the tubes are double-butted and are straight. Torque Tubes are fitted from rear of Frame to bottom of Engine support, in a very neat manner as shown.

FORKS.—Are of robust construction, and have been designed specially to meet the demands of this fast Machine. They impart a remarkable degree of comfort to the Machine, and there is no indication whatever of Front Wheel wobble in striking small bumps on the road. Lubrication is by Greasers which feed Spindles through Flats machined on them. Lamp Brackets are incorporated in the Fork design and are carried on the sprung portion. All Lugs, etc., for carrying internal expanding Front Wheel Brakes are stamped on part and parcel of the Fork.

HANDLEBARS.—Are 32" wide and are swept forward and out: they are arranged in an ideal position for comfortable riding. They are fitted with Rubber grips. Another type of bar, to be called No. 2, bringing grips 3in. higher and 2in. further back, are fitted when Machine is specified for Sidecar work. The following controls are fitted in the most convenient position to the rider's hands:—

LEFT BAR—Oiling lever, Clutch lever, Ignition lever.

RIGHT BAR—Front brake, Exhaust lifter, Carburettor controls.

The control wires are carried through special clips brazed on to the frame.

An original ad for the Brough Superior is both charming and beautiful. "The finish of all parts inside and out is superfine," the fine print reads. "The balance of this Special Super Engine is such that no vibration is appreciable at any engine speed."

More original ad copy for the Brough Superior: "Every SS 80' is guaranteed to be capable of exceeding 80 mph Solo and 65 mph with Sidecar."

During my research at the time, I had conversations with several people in the Brough club who had personally known George Brough and who knew Ike Webb, the factory foreman. They had all heard comments over the years about a "shop bike" that had been kept by the Brough works for more than five years.

Brough's brilliant engineer was a fellow named Harold Karslake; he was the guy who "made it happen" for his boss. He was a walking research and development department all to himself, and he's very famous in the Brough community. Karslake's personal papers had wound up in private hands, but I was able to secure them by spending an exorbitant amount of money (acquiring them was invaluable for documenting other Brough motorcycles I owned at the time).

In these ancient files were volumes of notes in Karslake's own hand. It took a while to sort through everything, but I finally found references to my 001 SS 100, such as when a 1925 to-do list included "fitting of shop SS 100 with 7" front brakes" and "sidecar brake on shop SS 100." The bike had been offered to the press originally with a skimpy 5" brake, but he updated it in 1925.

The World's Finest Rider

Solo 123 MILES PER HOUR
ON THE ROAD

Sidecar 103 MILES PER HOUR
ON THE ROAD

H. LE VACK ON HIS "BROUGH SUPERIOR"

has during the past eighteen months, using both "SS. 80." and "SS. 100" Models, won the 200 Miles Solo and Sidecar Races at Brooklands, creating Nine World's Records. At Arpajeon, near Paris, the above record speeds were put up which incidentally are the

HIGHEST SPEEDS EVER ACCOMPLISHED ON A MOTOR CYCLE

Private Owners riding their own "Ridden-on-the-road-every-day" "Brough Superiors" have been remarkably successful as shown by the following list of Principal Wins during the 1924 Season :—

LONDON TO EDINBURGH : 15 Starters gained 15 Gold Medals	SOUTH WESTERN CENTRAL TRIAL : Gold Medal	DUBLIN & DISTRICT M.C.C. : Jacobs Cup ; Walker Cup
2,500 MILE TRIAL ROUND GERMANY : Two Starters gained two Gold Shields	HUDDERSFIELD M.C.C. : Fastest Time of Day	DUBLIN M.C.C. : Dunlop Cup ; Freeman Cup ; Gold Medal.
LONDON TO LANDS END : Three Gold Medals	WELSH T.T. 100 MILE RACE AT PENDINE : Won in record time by Private Owner against all comers	BRADFORD M.C.C. : Fastest time of the Day ; Dyson Shield
SCOTTISH SIX DAYS : Silver Cup		Winner of ALL THREE 50 MILE RACES AT SOUTHPORT
BROOKLANDS 3 LAP HANDICAP : First	LEINSTER 2-DAY TRIAL : Silver Cup	(Second year in succession)

"GRAND PRIX OF BADEN" (AUSTRIA) 100 KILOMETRE RACE
WON BY ARCHDUKE WILHELM HAPSBURG

On The World's Finest Machine

More original ad copy for the Brough Superior: "Highest speeds ever accomplished on a motorcycle."

As for the sidecar reference, I realized the "shop SS 100" was not officially registered and was (illegally) driven on borrowed number plates. Photos of the bike and an attached sidecar appear in print in 1926 and 1927. From my research, I also believe the 001 motorcycle is the same one that Karslake won a gold medal on during the 400-mile London to Edinburgh race in 1926.

This was the clue I had been searching for. This cinched it for me. Karslake was talking about the bike Brough had kept for so many years before selling it—the prototype SS 100.

Since there is scant record of its existence before 1930, I can only speculate the 001 bike was sold because the Great Depression was squeezing the company dry. It is also likely that a six-year-old SS 100 was no longer useful as a press or development vehicle because so many improvements had been made on production models.

No matter the reason for its sale, the 001 is arguably a vehicle with an amazing degree of historic value—a fact that was not "discovered" until I read a 70-year-old shop diary.

I have to give special thanks to longtime Brough Machine Registrar Mike Leatherdale, who acknowledged in writing the references to the "shop bike" by former shop foreman Ike Webb, who stamped "001" on the frame to indicate it was the first SS 100 at the time of its 1930 sale. Leatherdale also confirmed "30726" as the earliest known engine for any SS 100 and that it was used by the works as a test bed, loan bike, and general hack and never properly registered during works ownership.

He also verified that "AU 7738" was the illegally used shop bike registration number as evidenced in photos from a *Motor Cycling* road test (January 7, 1925), Karslake's London-Edinburgh win (May 22, 1926), and a shot of it with a sidecar by a stone wall (March 1928).

ACKNOWLEDGMENTS

The toughest part of writing a book is remembering to thank everyone who gave a hand in getting it done. As usual, I have a bunch of thank yous, starting with a couple of guys who really helped me get this project finished because of my tendency to bite off more than I can chew.

Thanks to Brad Bowling, who used a few weeks before starting a new career with Auctions America to get this ready to print. Brad's name is on a few of the stories, but he is responsible for so much more. And Larry Edsall, my long-time writing buddy, who helped me finish up a couple of stories. I couldn't have done it without you guys.

Pat Simmons, my new-found friend from the Doobie Brothers, a life-long "picker," agreed to write the foreword. Pat, I'm so proud to know you and Cris.

The maestro, Dale Walksler, who with his son Matt, gave up untold days to walk me through and explain their bikes in the best collection of unrestored motorcycles on the planet – The Wheels Through Time Museum in Maggie Valley, North Carolina. Thank you once again, guys.

And to all the folks who helped me with leads and stories, including: The Crapoholic Brothers, Al and Ken Kelly, who always have a boatload of new barn-find stories to tell; Dicky Panuski; Lanny Hyde; Jason Belits; Jamie Waters; Mike Stenhouse; Chris Slawski; Somer Hooker; Buzz Kanter; Sam Bernstein; John Brutosky; John Stiner; Mark Supley; Carl Haren; Brian Keating; John Casteras; David White; Steve Geiger; Dave Minerva; Steve Barber; Lyle Manheimer; Rich Mooradian; Gregg Rammel; Rich Pollock; David Dammen; Brian Rankine; Michael FitzSimons; Carlos Escudero; Denver Cornett; Tom Hensley; Mark Mitchell; Mike Long; David White; Richard Pollack; David Dammen; Doug Kaufman; and Raymond Miller.

Thanks to my partners at Motorbooks International, Zack Miller and Jordan Wiklund who are always willing to listen to another one of my crazy book ideas. Thanks to all the book designers, editors, fact checkers and sales folks, who have helped make these books a success.

And of course to my wonderful wife Pat, who knows every time I sign another book contract, she loses her dining table for several months.

If I've left your name out of these acknowledgments, it's not because I didn't appreciate your involvement, it's just that I was too disorganized to write your name down.

Thank you for buying this book. If enough of you buy it, I'll write another one in a few years.

Cheerio,

Tom Cotter